A Psalm to My Sons
Written by Dr. Rory Brown-Sipp

First edition
"A Psalm to My Sons"
Copyright 2014 by Dr. Rory Brown-Sipp
Book Design and All Illustrations are Copyright 2014 by Dr. Rory Brown-Sipp
ALL RIGHTS RESERVED

This book may not be reproduced in its entirety or in part without written permission from the author, except for short passages that may be quoted for purposes of a book review or instructional use in a classroom or youth group setting; nor may any part of this book be reproduced mechanically or in digital form to be stored, transmitted, broadcast or otherwise retrieved without written permission from the author.

Concept for Book Cover and Chapter Illustrations by Dr. Rory Brown-Sipp
Graphic Design, Illustration Artwork, and Photo Composites by Ricky Scott Holmes
Photographs of Author by Quincy Nelson, EyeQphotography.com

Contact information for the author, book ordering details, and artwork reprint order forms can be found online at www.APsalmToMySons.com

Published by EISTEAM Consulting, Inc.
www.eisteamconsulting.com

This book is produced and printed entirely in the USA.

ISBN 10: 0-9899162-0-0
ISBN 13: 978-0-9899162-0-2

Categories:
1. Self-help/Personal Growth/Esteem. 2. Adolescent/Young Adult Nonfiction.
3. Spiritual Guidance. 4. Family and Relationships/Life Stages.

Disclaimer
"A Psalm to My Sons" was written to inspire and give insight, not to pass judgment or to dictate what its readers should consider right or wrong. The statements and inferences made in this book are based solely on the opinions of Rory Brown-Sipp, Ed.D., and what he personally considers useful guidance and important information, not best practice in the field of education and human development. Parental guidance is advised for readers under the age of 18.

The scriptural references that appear throughout the book are included for illustration and emphasis only and may be based on any one of the many assorted English versions or Bible translations—King James (KJV), New International (NIV), English Standard (ESV), New King James (NKJV), and possibly others; however, no selection was made to imply any preference for one version over another. The references are Christian-based without regard to any specific denomination.

# TABLE OF CONTENTS

Acknowledgements 6

About the Cover & Artwork 7

About the Author 8

Preface 10

CHAPTER ONE
Artwork Title: "Heritage"
Life Lesson 1: Son, Father, Man, Christian, Leader 15

The Son 15

The Father 16

The Man 18

The Christian 21

The Leader 24

Lessons Learned 27

CHAPTER TWO
Artwork Title: "Reflections"
Life Lesson 2: Becoming Who You Are 31

Lessons Learned 37

CHAPTER THREE
Artwork Title: "Boys Do Cry"
Life Lesson 3: Real Men and Boys Do Cry 41

Lessons Learned 43

CHAPTER FOUR
Artwork Title: "H.O.P.E - Hands of Peace & Empathy"
Life Lesson 4: Keep Cool. Communicate. Live Violence-Free 47

Lessons Learned 53

CHAPTER FIVE
Artwork Title: "Intimacy"
Life Lesson 5: Abstinence, Intimacy, and Avoiding "Baby Mama" Drama 57

Lessons Learned 63

CHAPTER SIX
Artwork Title: "Two Roads, One Dream"
Life Lesson 6: Education, Enterprise, and Empowerment 67

PAID Life System 73
Lessons Learned 75
Lessons from History: Honoring Civil Rights Pioneers 76

CHAPTER SEVEN
Artwork Title: "The Gift"
Life Lesson 7: The Gift of Christ 81

Lessons Learned 85

ADDENDUM

Reflections and Resolutions Guide 89

Reflections and Resolutions Worksheets

- Life Lesson 1 91
- Life Lesson 2 95
- Life Lesson 3 99
- Life Lesson 4 103
- Life Lesson 5 107
- Life Lesson 6 111
- Life Lesson 7 115

Stay Connected 119

Resources 120

Gallery of Artwork 123

Acknowledgements

In honor of some very strong men of valor who helped make me the man I am today.

Roy Anthony Brown, my father
Daddy, I love you!

John Douglas Sipp, my maternal grandfather
Enoch Brown Sr., my paternal grandfather
Your memory lives on through me.

My uncles Robert L. Sanders and Enoch Brown Jr.
Your lives ended too soon.

In honor of some very strong women of virtue in my life who have shaped the man I am today.

Brenda Joyce Sipp, my mother
I love you! You're an angel whose memory remains with me always.

Mrs. Hattie Mae Sipp, my maternal grandmother
Mrs. Fannie Mae Brown, my paternal grandmother
Your beautiful spirits will live on in my heart.

TO MY SON, RESHAUDE

This is for my only son, to whom I dedicate most of my works. Wherever you may go, always take a piece of me with you, along with the memory of my words and blessings for your life.
I love you with all of my heart!
And I am proud to acknowledge your newborn son,
Aiyden Reshaude (born 3/12/14)—my first grandchild!

MY THANKS

I acknowledge and thank my editing team
Parker Philpot and Maramis Choufani
for their advice and dedicated work.

I am grateful to Ricky Scott Holmes for his artistry and graphic design skills.

Thanks to KC Christon (Author, "Hang'n with Kasey" children's book series) for his assistance.

And special thanks to Toney W. Stephenson.

ABOUT THE COVER & ARTWORK

Starting with the cover, on through the illustrations in *A Psalm to My Sons*, every image captures a part of my life's experiences, reflects my viewpoints, and assists me with delivering lessons from my life's story in a more visual and artistic fashion. The artwork pays homage to the life lessons I've learned while living in the rural South—the essence of my childhood—through my career today. The cover imagery reflects passing on those lessons learned to the next generations, which I aspire to do with my readers.

Consider the artwork throughout the book to be the beautiful backdrops to my very colorful childhood and young adult experiences. Although I am not a design artist, I'm so thankful for having my old photograph collection, because those photos allowed me to share with my graphic artist many of the memorable landmarks, events, and places I recall from growing up in and around Birmingham, Alabama. Those images were inspiration for the artistic design of the book cover and other artwork created by Ricky Scott Holmes.

The little white church in the distance is an ever-fading building depicting my ever-increasing faith and spiritual connection to God. The street sign, Jaybird Road, is another personal reminder: It's the street I grew up on in the rural parts of Alabama, and it serves as a sign reminding me to keep a humble heart and to always cherish the wonderful experiences I had as a young man.

I want my readers to see at first glance that *Psalm* is a spiritual book of inspiration to be shared with young men of all ages, nationalities, and races. My hope for "my sons" is that each one clearly sees an image representative of his eager youthfulness, reaching out for knowledge and receiving motivational information shared openly from my past and present experiences. May each one see education and a good work ethic as a foundation for a stable, successful, future and stand upon an open book filled with caring words that may serve as grounding guidance for a lifetime.

The artwork from front to back is inspired by my family, my friends, my tears, my smiles, and my life!

Enjoy.

ABOUT THE AUTHOR
Dr. Rory Brown-Sipp

A Psalm to My Sons is Dr. Rory Brown-Sipp's first book and was inspired by his own life experiences. Psalm incorporates his spiritual insights and his desire to support America's youth, especially underserved, at-risk, young men of color.

At the time Dr. Sipp wrote this book, he was an instructor at the University of Nevada, Las Vegas (UNLV) and also served as the Executive Director for Acelero Learning, one of the largest providers of Head Start services in the state of Nevada.

In July 2012, Dr. Sipp was honored at the White House by President Barack Obama's administration as a White House Champion of Change for his outstanding dedication and devotion to his work in a social service program providing support to our nation's most vulnerable citizens.

Dr. Sipp has been in the fields of early childhood education and special education for over 20 years, during which time he served as an educator, an administrator, an author, a child and family advocate, and a Christian leader.

After completing a portion of his undergraduate studies at Faulkner University in Birmingham, Alabama, Dr. Sipp relocated to Las Vegas in 1998, where he completed his bachelor's in early childhood education and earned his master's in educational leadership, followed by his doctorate in special education, all at UNLV.

Dr. Sipp served as a member of several state, regional, and national boards, working with groups advocating for young children and families who live in poverty.

He is an active member at Alpha and Omega International Ministries under pastors Dr. Frank Gaston and Lady Rose Gaston.

Dr. Sipp has one son, Reshaude, who was born in their hometown of Birmingham.

Braylon Patton, Derryek Patton, Malik Scott Holmes, Isa-Hazem Macci Bajalia

PREFACE

Dedicated to All My Sons

In writing *A Psalm to My Sons*, I would be remiss if I did not first mention the influence of two great men in my life. These two men not only inspired me to write a self-help guide for young men of all races, nationalities, and cultures, but had a direct impact on who I have become today as a man, a father, and a Christian.

The men I am referring to are my Heavenly Father, Jesus Christ, and my earthly father, Roy Anthony Brown.

For more reasons than I could ever count, I give reverence to my Lord and Savior, Jesus Christ, for breathing life into me after making me from the substance of the earth, including me in His divine will, and leading me in this great work here on earth.

God has blessed me with and held me accountable for sharing the greatest gift of all—*love*—loving his people, people of all races, nationalities, and genders.

This book is a demonstration of my accountability and particularly my heartfelt desire to help at-risk, young men of color across the nation. Although I have only one biological son—Reshaude D. McCune, who was 21 around the time I started writing this book—many other young men have thought of me as a father.

God knew I would need an earthly role model to show me how to act as a young Black man, a son, a father, a citizen, and a leader. The Lord knew I would need a hardworking, sensitive, God-fearing, giving, family man who would be no stranger to providing for his family by the sweat of his brow. Therefore, He gave me my father. I know that one would think it would be the other way around since I am my father's son, but that's the way I see it.

My dad has been a great influence in my life and has been actively involved with me from the day I was born. It was his influence that encouraged me to "work smarter and not harder."

It was my dad's influence that encouraged me to be as present as I have always been in my own son's life. It was that same influence that taught me to hold myself accountable and to stand up like "a real man" to the consequences of all my actions.

The following seven chapters called Life Lessons are each followed by topical discussion summaries, or Lessons Learned, which address some of the most compelling issues faced by male adolescents and teenagers, and many young men: love and relationships, sexual risks and premature parenting, self-actualization and setting goals, gaining spiritual strength, non-violent communication, and walking a safe, healthy path through life's modern pitfalls.

Please use this book as a supplemental guide to what you may have learned from your parents, your culture, or your own life experiences; and definitely, use it parallel to your Bible readings or along with your spiritual instructional resources.

I hope with all my heart that something I have written may ignite you, my sons, to live a happier, more stress-free, and loving life, and I will carry that prayer in my heart always.

~Rory

CHAPTER ONE
Son, Father, Man, Christian, Leader

"Heritage"
INSPIRED BY: DR. RORY BROWN-SIPP   ILLUSTRATED BY: RICKY SCOTT HOLMES

LIFE LESSON 1
Son, Father, Man, Christian, Leader

The Son

I was born in 1972, a time when Black people in America were fighting to advance, contributing to the nation, yet struggling to integrate and become an accepted part of American society. It was a time when African-American men and woman were also just striving for day-to-day survival despite the oppressive conditions such as those present in the Deep South, particularly in my birthplace, Birmingham, Alabama.

Racial segregation was still prevalent in the early '70s, bigotry was everywhere, and few places were safe for Black families. Even by that point in our nation's history it still was not safe for children to worship in their own local churches without fear of being attacked; it had been a decade since four little girls were killed in a hateful bombing at the 16th Street Baptist Church in my hometown.

It was a crazy time but through it all, Black families continued to depend on God and one another and prayed that a change would soon come. It was also a time when people embraced love—love for living, love for peace, and love for one another.

It was during this same time that my mother and father connected on their life paths in Birmingham. They met, fell in love, and married in the early '70s.

My dad, then 22, had recently been honorably discharged from the United States Marine Corps, and my mother, then 25, was working in the medical field as a technician at one of the local hospitals.

My mother was an extremely beautiful woman. She was fair-skinned, with beautiful brown eyes, and had dimples that accompanied her smile, which could light up the darkest of rooms. Her inner beauty was even more pronounced than her outer beauty. She was a reserved woman of very few words, yet very articulate when she did speak.

My father—loving, compassionate, sensitive, and very analytical—was tall, dark, and handsome, with an athletic, 6-foot-tall physique, and a very strong presence.

Nowadays, when I look in the mirror, I'm often surprised at the *me* I see. Some days I look like my mother; at other times, I am the spitting image of my father. On top of having their obvious physical genes, I can see that I inherited many of their ways.

From my mother, I get my more reserved temperament, often being a man of few words. Although when I do have to speak out, it is tempered by my father's compassionate, thoughtful qualities—most of the time.

I attribute much of my overall character to the attributes I inherited from my mother and father. I wasn't always the person I've grown to become, but after gaining a better understanding of my family and personal history, I appreciate being who I am today.

The Father

When I was 16 years old, I was a freshman at the local community college in Birmingham, Alabama, along with my best friend and high school sweetheart, Leslie. She and I looked forward to sharing a bright future: she wanted to become a nurse, and I wanted to become a computer information specialist. We talked about getting married and having children—when the time was right. That was the plan.

For that time period, around the beginning of the 1990s, the socioeconomic factors in that rural area and cultural influences had more or less determined that the "right time" for parenting was when teenagers were still in high school. Sadly, it had become a trend of children making children. It was the norm to see students between the ages of 15 and 18 having babies.

Now that I am older, I realize that something extremely important was missing from our early schooling: sex education. Classes where reproductive health, abstinence, and responsible parenting would have been discussed were nonexistent.

However, at my former high school, a teen mothers program was implemented in order to support the high number of girls who wanted to complete high school and not drop out because of pregnancy. New mothers could bring their children to school and continue with their regular curriculum, while another part of the day would be spent learning hands-on parenting techniques in a separate area for child care.

Sex education remained absent from our curriculum, even though the number of teen pregnancies at our high school continued to increase. The teen mothers program did continue until the time I graduated from high school in 1989 but, unfortunately, there was nothing to educate male teens about the risks of having sex too early and parenting too soon.

Although the pressure to fit in with the culture at my school during that time was nearly overwhelming, I made a vow that I would not father a child while still a child myself—or at least not while I was in high school. I also vowed to focus on getting my education and graduating from high school just as my older siblings, Robby and Rhonda, had done several years earlier.

The rest of my high school years passed without my fathering any children because of my commitment to graduate, which I did as one of the top five of my graduating class.

After I graduated from high school, decided that I had already found my wife-to-be, and determined she would be a perfect mother, I felt I was ready to become a responsible parent with Leslie. One might think, "How could a 17-year-old even begin to know what *responsible* parenting means?"

That's the point: I didn't know and no one had told me.

You see, my sons, although being a father to my son, Reshaude, has been one of the best experiences of my life, my decision to become a parent was premature and I was ill-informed. It was premature because I was too young; I was ill-informed because of the reluctance that educators and parents had about discussing sex, sexually-transmitted diseases, responsible parenting, abstinence, and other sex-oriented topics.

I wish someone would have stopped long enough to have that difficult but important conversation with me regarding safe sex and the impact of what would happen when a young man has unprotected sex and a pregnancy results. I also would have wanted to learn about caring for a baby, how marriage works, and how to gain financial stability as well.

Silence about those important things was the norm for adults back then (and, too frequently, it still is). Responsible adults ought to inform young men about the realities of teen parenting to help them avoid getting involved in sex before they are ready for the undesired consequences. Also, there are risks to premature sex other than pregnancy that ought to be discussed before it is too late, especially sexually transmitted diseases, of which HIV can lead to AIDS and often causes premature death.

If over the years there had been more self-help guides—similar to this one—more young men could have been better informed about sexuality, ways to avoid pregnancy, and how to make better relationship decisions for a more successful life.

When my son was born, I didn't get a guide for how to be a good father. However, it was my desire to do things the best way I could that inspired me to educate myself on the best principles and appropriate practices for parenting. It was my desire to engage in responsible parenting by becoming a loving and accountable father. That meant that regardless of how young I was, *I was someone's father.*

Regardless of how limited my funds were at that time, I realized my money had to be shared with someone who had a greater need than my own.

Regardless of the mistakes I made in life, it was my responsibility to try to steer my son away from the same or similar mistakes, discouraging him from following in my footsteps down the wrong path. Over the years, I practiced asking my son open-ended questions to encourage conversation with him and to allow him to use his expressive language.

I preferred to talk with him about the consequences of his inappropriate actions; I reinforced his appropriate actions with praise, and I chose to refrain from using corporal punishment.

I was so relieved when my son turned 21 and still had his youthfulness, his life ahead of him, and his freedom as a single man—without the responsibility of children. I felt confident that he got all the lessons I taught him about abstinence, safe sex, healthy intimate relationships, and becoming a responsible parent—but only when the time is right.

It's good to feel like a responsible father!

The Man

Looking back over my early life, I recall my journey from boyhood to manhood—real manhood. For most of us, that journey starts in our young minds first, mistakenly thinking we have become a "real man" long before we actually are.

My sons, it is funny how a teenage boy often looks for reasons to support his saying, "I am a man now." At around 16 years old, he will typically look at one or more visible signs to decide he has moved from boyhood to manhood.

Initially, he may look at his own appearance. He'll look closely at his face to find facial hair—so-called peach fuzz—as soon as it may start to appear. Based simply on that faint presence of a moustache or a vague-looking beard, some boys instantly begin to equate their outward *appearance of masculinity* with manliness. For some boys, that one little enhancement to the physical appearance, perhaps along with a deepening voice, leads them to try to act as if they are already grown men.

As a boy reaches 18 or so and his facial hair may be more defined—there could also be chest hair showing—he then more strongly asserts, "I'm a real man!" However, the only thing that has changed about his life is mainly his physical development.

As time rolls on, young males continue to change physically in many ways, but still they are boys. The things they may choose to do and activities they participate in may be driven mainly by their inexperience, youth, and lack of understanding about consequences because they are still boys.

Then, society opens new doors for growing boys to participate legally in a variety of activities as they reach certain ages. At 18, he may be able to vote in many jurisdictions, and he can sign his own contracts at that "age of majority" under the law.

At last, there are some "adult" privileges made available at age 21. You know, the usual ones that come with a 21st birthday. Depending upon which state and local ordinances apply, cigarettes and liquor can be purchased legally at stores; adults can go into nightclubs where smoking and drinking are commonplace, and adult-rated materials are legally accessible.

This is what some young men have been anticipating for years, believing that these activities go hand-in-hand with being a real man. These new enticements may be the factors behind his thinking, "I'm really a man now!" Really? The only things that have changed at this point for the man-wannabe are his appearing older and having more age-based privileges. If he thinks he's a man, his circumstances might say otherwise.

Ask if this "real man" is still sleeping in that same bed in his parents' home. Is he still eating food from the parents' refrigerator and pantry? What amount of money is he contributing to help pay the household bills—lights, water, cable, phone, and so on? It is probably little to not nearly enough.

That's what far too many young males do—not enough. Sadly, they are allowed to continue doing very little when the parents or some other adult rewards that bad behavior by financing the cigarette, drinking, and partying habits of that "man," which only enables him to stay immature. Now this is not the case in every household, but growing up in my community, I found it to be the case in most situations.

As I grew older, I was prone to doing some immature thinking. Even though the legal adult age for most purposes was 21, and even though I was a father at 17 years old, and even though I had graduated from high school in 1989 and was in my second year of college—I was still a kid.

I thought the world revolved around me. I had entitlement issues. I thought I should ask and it should be given unto me with little or no effort on my part. Yep, I was a man, right? Wrong! It was those actions and that way of thinking that truly illustrated to me and to others that I was a little, self-centered, egotistical boy!

Then suddenly, my main support system at home went away—my mother, my maternal grandmother, and my grandfather all passed away, one right after the other from 1989 to 1991, when I was between 15 and 17, basically leaving me on my own. I was still a kid struggling to become a man.

In a few years, I began to identify what real men looked like; I observed the kinds of things they accomplished, how they behaved, and whose respect they earned. After several more years had passed, my eyes and my mind were open to more revelations and divine wisdom.

I came to accept that Life was doing what it was designed to do. It was designed to give birth just as quickly as it was designed to make room for death. The earth was designed to rotate on its axis; it was created to keep on moving, just as time changes by the second or even faster. I learned that every action had a reaction and a consequence.

Most important of all, I acknowledged that it was time for me to stop thinking about what I could get and to start thinking about how I could give.

First, how could I give to myself? I needed advanced education, a career, finances, a meaningful way of life, and more. How could I provide better for my son—as a father should? Beyond that, how could I give back to society?

I wanted to become a productive citizen, as well as demonstrate good stewardship and responsibility. It was critical for me to develop good leadership for the sake of my family and others.

These are some of the duties of a "real man."

A real man takes full responsibility for his own life and for every child he helps bring into this world. I realized that a real man knows when it's time to get out of the bed provided by his parents and find a nesting place of his own. But if your circumstances make it necessary for you to remain in their home, you ought to pay your own way and pull your own weight by contributing to the upkeep and operations of that household. A real man looks for opportunities to assist his parents and for ways to contribute financially to help them in return for their support.

My mother and my aunt would often say, "Every tub must stand on its own bottom," which means that we each must be accountable as men and not rely on others for support.

My sons, being a man takes time, effort, and wisdom. I found that I really didn't truly become a man until I was almost 24 years old.

Something wonderful happened to me the day I knew I had finally become a man, and after I read **Corinthians 13:11**: *"When I was a child, I talked like a child, I thought like a child, I reasoned like a child. When I became a man, I put childish ways behind me."* I turned selfless, putting Jesus first, my son and family second, and I got in line somewhere after them.

My sons, when I stepped into manhood, I stopped "busting a sag" with my pants hanging off my butt and began to embrace every reason why I should wear the pants "upright and tight." I could wear my pants the right way because I worked and paid my own way, and I was a good provider for my family.

I began to make good decisions, the kind that would have a positive impact and favorably influence my life and my destiny for many years to come. Wow, it feels good to be able to truthfully say, "I *am* a real man."

The Christian

So far, my sons, I have been transparent about practically every aspect of my life. I have given you background information regarding my conception; I have provided intricate details on my journey into manhood; and I've given you particulars about my experiences with parenting. I think it would also be most appropriate to share with you how I became a Christian and who I am as a Christian today.

One thing I know for certain: I am a Christian. I believe in the birth, death, and resurrection of Jesus Christ. I believe He died for my sins and my salvation, and I believe He rose again because He is a true and living God.

I was a Christian even before I was born: anointed by God and filled with the Holy Ghost while still in my mother's womb. I am certain I jumped around with joy, kicked and stomped on the devil's head, and screamed out praises to God at every opportunity.

I had no choice but to be a Christian; it was in my DNA. My mother was a Christian, her mother was a Christian, and my grandmother's mother was a Christian. See, it's in my genes! However, I didn't always operate or function as a Christian when I was younger. I had not yet made Christianity a lifestyle.

My lifestyle was focused on being cool, being with the "in crowd," and remaining fashionable. Although my parents introduced me to Christ a long time ago, while I was still a boy, I did not see or make the real connection for myself. I knew that I loved the Lord, but as I soon learned, God was not one to be played with. I feared Him and knew I needed to go to church every Sunday to worship Him because my mother told me so—but I still couldn't make the real connection.

I eventually had somewhat of a revelation, at about 10 or 11 years old, about connecting with God and staying active in church. It was a bright and sunny Sunday morning in Birmingham, Alabama.

I was sitting in church all geared up to hear the gospel singers. The singing in a

Southern Baptist church was amazing (and that was really my primary reason for attending church). However, as time progressed, I soon discovered I had a secondary reason for attending. It was the beautiful sight of a very attractive young lady that we called "Niecy."

Niecy was light-skinned with sandy brown hair and cat eyes—green or grey in color. She was petite, had a beautiful personality, and she loved the Lord. Her mother was the choir director, and her brothers played instruments for the choir. Niecy was everything a young boy could dream of, and eventually she became my first girlfriend.

At 10 or 11 years old, there isn't much dating or courtship going on and definitely no quiet moments alone. However, there was a neutral ground, a meeting place where we could see each other: it was the church.

That was it—I could see her at church! With that in mind, my sporadic Sundays transitioned into every Sunday and my Sunday-only visits led me to attend Vacation Bible School. Then, guess what? I even joined the choir. (I told you I loved the Lord. Okay, I also became fond of Niecy.) I didn't know it, and I don't think Niecy knew it either, but she was a conduit for bringing me even closer to God back then, which led to who I am now as a Christian.

I found myself attending church frequently even after she left our church to attend services elsewhere, which was long after our puppy love had ended. I found myself reading the Bible more often and attending church regularly. I remained an active member of the choir as I still am to date. However, I still had not made my deeper, more abiding connection with God at that time.

It wasn't until I began to face adversities, challenges, depression, and disappointments; it wasn't until I needed to experience a great move of God in my life that I really became connected and really stepped up to being a devout Christian—the kind of Christian who operated under His guidance and His will.

During one particularly difficult period in my life, I wondered if Jesus really did exist. I was 17, and my mother—who was only 43—passed away suddenly, in 1990. She had a massive heart attack while she was providing child care for my son so I could attend school. I was a student at the local community college, and according to her death certificate, I was only minutes away from our house, heading to school, when it hit her.

In writing this section, a lot of memories came up for me. I just could not comprehend how my mother could have died from a heart attack at such a young age. How could my mother die?

I didn't know it then, but my mother died so that I could live. That sounds kind of weird, huh? Well, it's the revelation I got years after my mother was deceased.

It's all in the numbers. God showed me that my mother's passing at 43 was her cycle of completion as assigned by Him.

God's perfect number is 7 (4+3=7), which in biblical sense means completion. Even more notable, I was 17 years old when my mother passed (1+7=8). Biblically, the number 8 means a new beginning, and that time in my life truly was a new beginning for me.

God clearly showed me that while my mother lived on earth—and while I depended solely on her—I had not learned to depend on Him. I found myself being guided by my parents and not by the voice of God. I had not yet found my life and my place in Christ, so I was actually spiritually dead! However, by the grace of God, I came to my senses.

I realized that I needed Him to ease my pain from my mother's death and to ease the pain I felt from my grandmother's passing just three months after my mother's death. They both passed away in the home in which they raised me and my siblings. For me, as a 17-year-old, it was so painful.

I just wanted God to stop the pain. I wanted Him to show me His favor and simply just have mercy upon me. I soon realized that God will allow whatever it takes to get our attention and to have us commune with only Him. He wants to hear from us. He wants us to acknowledge that He is Lord of Lords and King of Kings.

It was through my adversities, heartaches, and disappointments that I finally made my strongest connection to God. It wasn't my mother that made the connection; it wasn't a beautiful young woman that made the connection; it was my desire to be saved, to be set free, and to live life abundantly that caused me to cry out to Jesus and become saved.

I began to thirst for Jesus. I wanted to read more about Him and His word. I wanted to develop a more intimate relationship with Him, so I learned to pray. I wanted to show Him my appreciation, so I praised Him and worshiped Him; I wanted to show God I was obedient and that he could trust me with His financial money blessings, so I made certain to give my tithes and offerings.

As I became more rooted in Christ and learned to trust Him more, I learned even more profound ways to worship. As I prayed, I began to get on my knees more often in reverence to God; when I really wanted an answer and a great move of God in my life, I would lay prostrate before him. I don't know what it is about that one act of humility, but it is extremely powerful. And, my sons, it surely brings forth results.

It feels good to be a Christian!

The Leader

I have often heard the adage, "Leaders are born and not made." I would beg to differ. In my opinion, the concept of being a "born leader" is a questionable one. That expression implies that unless you were born with the genetic makings of a leader, whatever that would entail, you could never choose to do the work in your life to become a leader.

My own life experiences have shown me that any of us can take steps to learn, practice, and achieve leadership. But first, in order to become an effective leader, it requires training, discipline, and passion for helping others; it requires more than knowledge and popularity.

When I first heard the old saying about "born leaders," I was around 15 years old. I thought I was knowledgeable, knew everything, and had all the answers for anyone who asked. That made me a "leader," right?

At that age, I was a fairly good student and had lots of book learning, but I had not yet learned an important adage that I've since come to believe real leaders know: "People don't care how much you know until they know how much you care."

From the sixth grade through my senior year in high school, I was definitely popular among the student body. My teachers liked me, my friends admired me, and in high school, I won the majority vote as class president. During my senior year, I was even voted Best Dressed and Most Likely to Succeed.

With those accolades and that recognition from my peers and others, I must have been quite a leader—born leader—wouldn't you think? Was I actually a born leader? Well, for me, the answer is no.

Although I don't believe true leaders are simply born that way, I do, however, believe there's a genetic predisposition that may influence or support a person's behavior and personality—which does not necessarily include his capacity to become a successful leader. I may have been popular in school, but that alone is not the key to leadership.

Along the way, I realized something fundamental about leadership: Many people liked me, but I didn't sense that many people *respected* me. At times when I engaged in inappropriate activities, such as cursing, gossiping, or worse, I didn't even respect myself. Therefore, *if no one respected me, I couldn't consider myself a leader.*

As I experienced life through my transitions from boy to father to man to leader —finally emerging into the full faith in God and the Christ-centered leadership I practice today—I worked to develop my character each step of the way.

I eventually learned effective ways of interacting with others and developed tools and methods that could help them feel more empowered to become successful. Others have shared with me how I served as their role model and a catalyst for their positive change.

As I began to empathize with others, they empathized with me in return. I earned the respect of men and women of varying ages, races, and nationalities by first respecting myself and never compromising my respect for mankind.

People started trusting in my intentions, knowledge, and abilities to be a leader at work, in church, and in my social circles. I had finally become a leader.

My sons, you can choose to rely only upon any innate leadership potential you think you have, or you can make a decision to learn to do what good leaders do, thereby becoming one yourself. Either way, it does not happen automatically—and certainly not by the luck of anyone's birth.

I can attest to just how much life experiences, exposure, training, and learning through trial and error are essential factors that go into building one's leadership skills and career.

I have dedicated my life to working in the social service industry where I have been afforded the opportunity to both lead others and to work under the leadership of some great people who earned their designation of leader through receiving the respect of others.

In my profession, I have served in many leadership capacities. Currently, I serve as the executive director for one of the largest and most successful Head Start programs—Acelero Learning, a Las Vegas-based, federally funded program that assists children and families with low income. During my tenure, it has always been my ultimate goal to positively affect the lives of individuals and their families, to inspire them to do greater things.

As I have discovered, my work has not gone unnoticed. Of the many local and national awards I have received over the years for my service and scholarship, perhaps the one I feel most honored by was received on June 18, 2012, at a White House ceremony, where I was recognized as one of eleven White House Head Start Champions of Change by President Barack Obama.

My sons, I have learned that we will not always know when our work is being observed and evaluated. We must strive to do our best through self-improvement and continue to advance in our lives. Our rewards will come from others who respect and value what we do that helps them to improve their lives. This is what leaders do.

THE WHITE HOUSE

WASHINGTON

July 5, 2012

Mr. Rory Sipp
North Las Vegas, Nevada

Dear Rory:

Congratulations on being selected as a White House Champion of Change. Thank you for the work you do every day.

From the earliest days of our founding, our Nation has been shaped by ordinary people who have dared to dream and used their unique skills to do extraordinary things. Americans like you help carry this tradition forward by reaching for new ideas that will help our country win the future. You and your fellow Champions embody the change you want to see in the world. Together, we will out-innovate, out-educate, and out-build the rest of the world to keep our country strong.

Congratulations, again, and I wish you all the best in your future endeavors.

Sincerely,

[signature]

A successful leader has self-respect and feels good about being of service to society. Regardless of any honors, awards, or recognition I receive, my greatest reward has always been—and will always be—the personal satisfaction and joy I get from teaching those who are eager to learn and being in a position to inspire those who will become future leaders.

1

Lessons Learned

Become a real man. Being a "real man" is going beyond being cool. Real men are accountable, responsible, and contribute to society. Becoming a "real man" begins when you shift your thinking from what you can get, to a mindset of what you can give.

Be accountable before becoming a parent. Hold yourself accountable for being well-informed about responsible parenting and adulthood before even considering parenting a child.

Live your life as a Christian. Becoming a Christian is about accepting God as your savior and about developing a personal relationship with Him as He influences you daily. Christianity is a lifestyle. The same way it is essential for you to have food, clothing, shelter, and physical fitness, it is essential that you have spiritual guidance and covering in your life; you can't live without it.

For more guidance, now turn to this Lesson's "Reflections and Resolutions" in the Addendum.

CHAPTER TWO
Becoming Who You Are

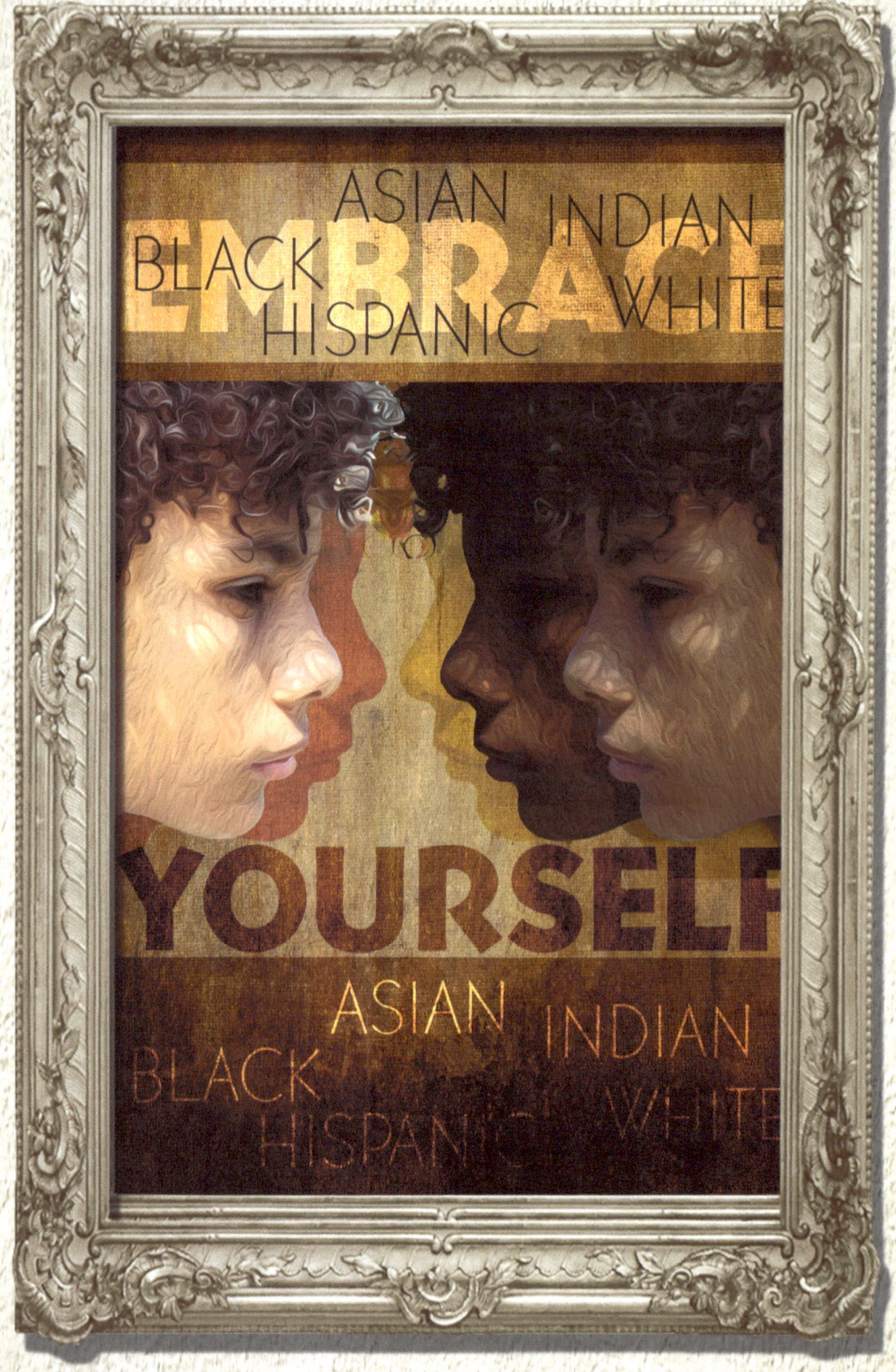

"Reflections"
INSPIRED BY: DR. RORY BROWN-SIPP   ILLUSTRATED BY: RICKY SCOTT HOLMES

LIFE LESSON 2
Becoming Who You Are

My sons, this chapter is all about you. It's all about recognizing the specific, special qualities you have as a person and realizing your worth even as you continue to build your own character. I do understand that it is not always easy to become comfortable in your own skin.

You would think it would be a piece of cake since you were born in your skin and have lived in it all your life. However, it's not easy because most of us tend to be overly self-critical—feeling inadequate in many ways, always believing others are better, and constantly making self-putdowns.

We can be our own worst critic.

From the time we wake up in the morning, we start our self-judgments. You wouldn't be the only young man who has stood in front of his mirror and said:

My skin is not smooth enough...
I'm not tall enough...
My complexion is not the right color...
I don't have enough facial hair...
My nose is too big...
I'm not handsome enough...
My muscles aren't defined enough...
I'm not strong enough...

Then, we walk out of our homes into an environment that feels like we are in a world-wide arena surrounded by countless judges of men, and we hear harsh criticisms that confirm what we have already decided about our personal appearance.

We allow the world around us—what we see in movies or read in digital media and print magazines—to dictate how we should look, how we should act, and how we should feel, forgetting that only the Creator who made us can sit in judgment of who we are.

But too often we feel that we don't measure up to the images in the media, which are usually unrealistic, unattainable, and often unhealthy. Typically, you see the televison commercials that illustrate how young men's bodies should look, or you see comments across social media, photos in magazines, and movie scenes that promote stereotypes.

Illustrations show young men with flawlessly airbrushed complexions; muscle-bound males with flat, six-pack abs; tough-looking guys with tattoos from head to toe; and others wearing high-priced shoes, jewelry, and high-fashion apparel.

Furthermore, these stereotypes show young men dressed in whatever happens to be the latest so-called fashion, whether it's "busting a sag," wearing bling-bling jewelry, or walking around in highly overpriced designer sneakers. Why?

Primarily, advertisers want to make you and your peers buy those products so they can make their big profits. The point is to make you feel the *need* to wear, own, or do certain things in order to fit in or to feel good about yourself. No outside influence in the world should have that much control over any of us.

What a way to brainwash you, my sons! *Don't let the media fool you.*

Think back and see if you can recall the last time you saw a commercial that illustrated what a respectful young man should look like. We don't see many media images or ads that clearly promote the characteristics of a young man with integrity, and rarely do we see the media illustrate a young man who loves the Lord. I can tell you, I have yet to see one.

All of the negative imagery is only a trick of the enemy to distract you, and if you are not aware, it will eventually throw you off track, hold you back, and take you out. It can hold you back in life and keep you wandering around in the wilderness of failure.

Ultimately, it can take you out by leaving you vulnerable to turning your life over to violence, gangs, and crime, or to using drugs as a way to escape feeling bad about yourself. The worst thing is that it can keep you from receiving God's blessings or realizing His promise for your life.

My sons, instead of trying to imitate the false images, decide on your *own* personal style. Make your own decisions and, above all, *be yourself.*

It took me many years to become comfortable in my own skin, so I can understand your struggles. In fact, I can share a few episodes and illustrations of how I found myself affected by outside criticism that influenced how I should look.

When I was in my early twenties I wanted to be an actor or a model. I just wanted to be famous! I would find myself looking in the mirror and hating what I saw.

I felt I wasn't light-skinned enough, I wasn't slim enough, I wasn't tall enough, and I just didn't look good enough. So, the reality of that dream seemed out of my reach—at that time.

Oh, my Lord! That brings back a crazy teenage memory regarding my height. There was a particular girl that I simply adored. Her skin tone was fairly light in color—what we in the Deep South historically called "high yellow." She had a nice shape and a good personality—or so I thought. I wanted to be her boyfriend so badly even though she didn't want to be my girlfriend. However, she said I could be her boyfriend under one condition: I could be her boyfriend *only* if I were "taller."

See what I mean? The judgment of the world… taller!? How could I possibly become taller overnight or in time to become her boyfriend? Well, I'd heard that if you hold on to a chin-up bar, hanging there for long periods of time, you would get taller by stretching your skin and bones. Dumb! (Did I mention I was only 13 or 14 years old at the time? Still, it was dumb!) I can tell you that plan didn't work, and thank God it didn't because had it worked, I would be with a shallow woman who couldn't appreciate a shorter man.

Then there was that other time in my life when I wanted a lighter complexion—even to look like a White person. That's not a good feeling to have—not in the sense that anything is wrong with being White, but in the sense that I did not value who I was as a Black person. Obviously I did not yet see the value in being comfortable in my own darker skin. I even remember bleaching my skin at one point in time—that was over 20 years ago.

Today there are talk shows featuring young Black girls who have engaged in the same unhealthy behavior I did and it is noble of them to share their stories; but my sons need the same type of stories told to them. I don't mind exposing myself to benefit all of you because I love you and care about you. I really want you to embrace who you are, my sons.

I'm almost certain I wasn't born wanting to change my appearance; there had to be some environmental factor that influenced such a desire or thought. Wow, it was just in that moment that I again recalled my beautiful mother, who already had a very light shade of skin; yet she too for some unknown reason wanted to be even lighter. She gave in to that desire by using some brand of skin-lightening cream. Ah! The influence of the world!

As life progressed and I became older, I realized that since my skin and I were a permanent pair, and since we would be sharing this life together, I should begin to embrace who I am, respect from where I've come, and love how I look and how I engage with the world.

There were other episodes that also influenced the way I thought I should act or behave. I thought as a young man—or a man in general—that I needed to be tough; I shouldn't cry because I would be called "weak," a "sissy," or a "cry baby." (In a different Life Lesson, I share some insightful and encouraging information with you regarding *crying* and why it is both normal and appropriate to engage in it.)

Several things then happened that directly influenced my decision to embrace who I am. First, I gave my life to Christ and I reminded myself that I am beautifully and wonderfully made in His image. In other words, whatever my race, nationality, or skin color, to God be the glory! Secondly, after fully, unconditionally, giving my life to Christ at around 33 years old, I began to respect from where I've come. And since then, I have never kept it a secret.

I am an American-born, Black man who was raised in the Deep South after being born at a hospital in Birmingham, Alabama. I could also be called a country man since my upbringing from birth until I was well into my teen years took place in a small, rural area where I lived in a town called Brighton, Alabama with my family. I lived with my mother, my maternal grandparents, and two of my siblings.

Although my father and I did not live in the same home after he and my mother divorced, I credit them both for helping me connect with my emotions and to be unafraid of showing my sensitivity. My siblings taught me the importance of unconditional love and why we each had the responsibility of showing such love to each other.

My grandmother, who we called "Madea" (Mother Dear), taught me not to be afraid to speak my mind, and she taught me by her example how to love the Lord. My grandfather taught me the power of listening and helped me understand the blessing of being a giver.

I didn't attend the best schools, but I had the best teachers. They loved me, disciplined me, and held me accountable. I was not a jock. I didn't play sports, but I played the drums in the band. I wasn't a straight-A student and, at times, I misbehaved in school.

I had to sit down one day and just embrace all of that. That's where I've come from; that's part of my life. Those were the most notable influences that shaped my thoughts and guided my behavior, which helped me become the man I am today.

Lastly, in embracing *me*, I began to fully accept and even love how I looked. One day, I just reconciled myself to certain facts: I will never be my teenage weight again; my skin is the color and shade it is; also, I finally left it up to God how tall I would be. (Little did I know it would be harder to find the right fit in clothes once you grow to six feet or more.)

Somewhere along the way, I realized that I was not the smartest person on this planet, but I was willing to learn more and more each day by reading regularly, listening often, and staying in school to further my formal education. I followed through, graduated with a bachelor's degree, and eventually earned my Ed.D. in Special Education. I realized that life's trials can only make me stronger as a person, stronger in the Lord, and stronger in my character.

Respect and embrace yourself

Building your character is embracing and respecting who you are as a person. It's about embracing your culture, your values, and your spirituality.

Your character is then molded from that foundation as you begin to understand and maintain integrity (doing the right thing even when no one is looking). Your character is then maintained by respecting yourself and others at all times, and respecting yourself enough to protect your body—which is your temple.

Respect your body enough to keep it free from drugs, alcohol, and spiritual poisons to the highest degree possible; protect your anointing (God's spiritual presence within you) by not frequenting places that are spiritually unclean. When you package acceptance of the body that God has given you, along with embracing your roots—both of which go into building your character—you will be on your way to becoming the authentic YOU.

My sons, you must embrace who you are because there can only be one *you*. You have been perfectly designed and destined for one purpose, but for many reasons. Your purpose is to love and serve God. And one of the main reasons you exist is to become a productive and contributing member of society here on the face of this place we call Earth.

2

Lessons Learned

Embrace who you are and learn to feel comfortable as you are. Be confident that you are wonderfully designed and made by God, so appreciate your unique self.

Stay above being manipulated or controlled by misleading, unhealthy, false images in the world. Be aware of how commercial media images and stereotypes are promoted and the ways they can negatively affect your sense of self-confidence. Don't allow those things to determine your destiny.

Develop your own personal style, but be mindful of your appearance and what it says about you. Even if something is in fashion, it may not be the look that's best for you.

Value the life experiences and trials that build character. Continue to shape who you are as a young man, and conduct yourself responsibly in the world.

Respect yourself and others in all ways and at all times.

For more guidance, now turn to this Lesson's "Reflections and Resolutions" in the Addendum.

CHAPTER THREE
Real Men and Boys Do Cry

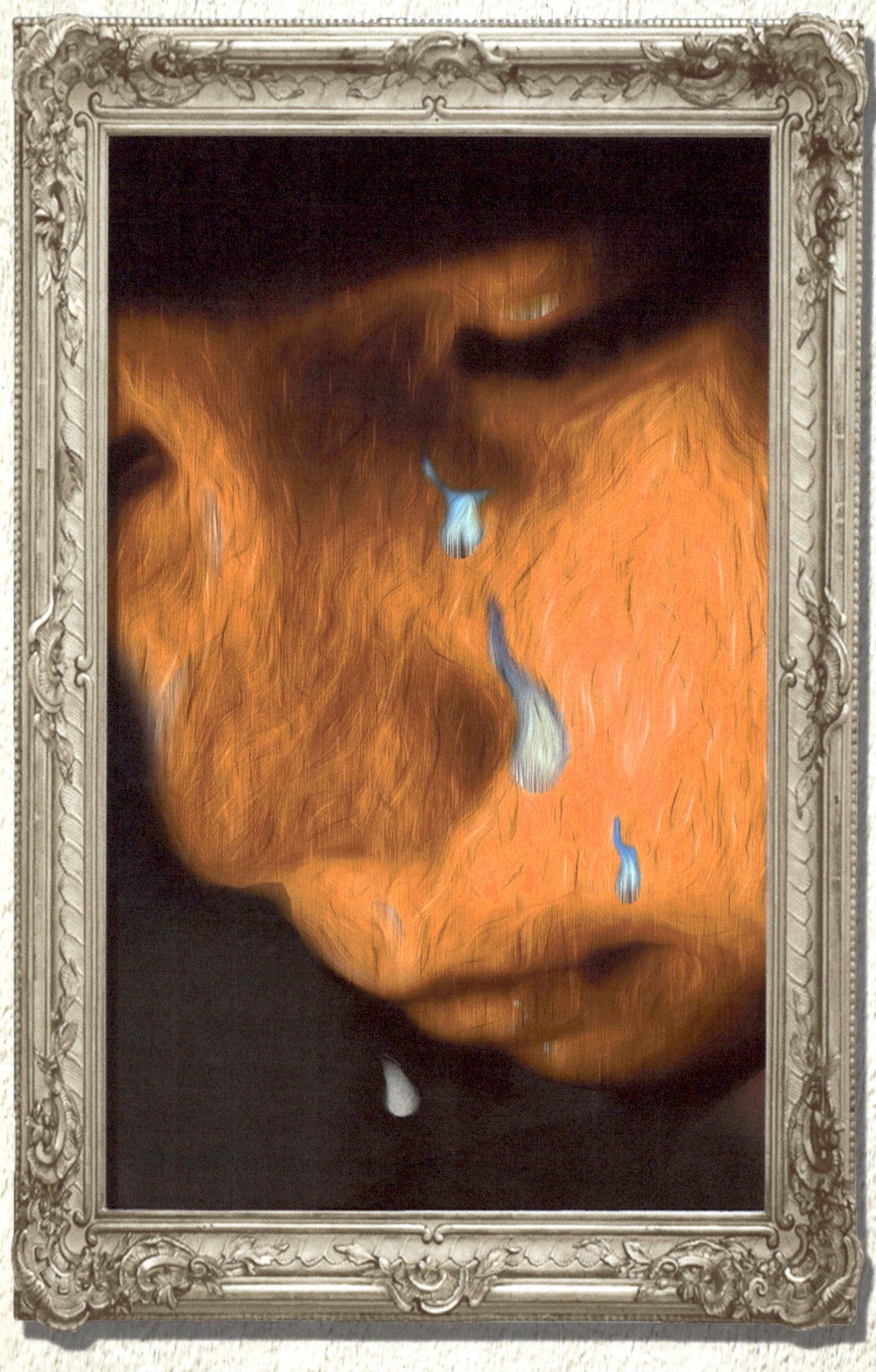

"Boys Do Cry"
INSPIRED BY: DR. RORY BROWN-SIPP   ILLUSTRATED BY: RICKY SCOTT HOLMES

LIFE LESSON 3
Real Men and Boys Do Cry

"Stop all of that crying!" "Tough it up!" "Look at you… crying like a little girl!" Those are only some of the many reprimands I heard all around me while I was growing up. Sadly enough, some 30 years later, I still hear men and woman telling their sons the same thing today.

My sons, this life lesson is all about helping you embrace and become comfortable with "crying," which is one of the many biological, self-soothing functions and expressions of the emotions we feel. There are many men, both young and old, who really believe you compromise your manhood and your masculinity when you shed a few tears. They actually believe you should be put out of the "Club of Masculinity" when you cry your heart out.

Who made this rule, and when is someone going to be brave enough to stop this foolishness? Well, I feel it is my responsibility to teach boys—and even men—a lesson on crying to help them understand that it is definitely okay to cry a little and to embrace their sensitivity.

I believe I am one of the best people to talk about this subject because I have mastered crying. Seriously! I cry at weddings, funerals, movies, and even when I hear a good love song that reminds me of the good ol' times.

How did I get so comfortable with crying? Why wasn't I programmed *not* to cry, and why didn't I simply decide to "tough it up" and "be a man"? Well, it definitely wasn't because society taught me it was okay to cry.

Early on, I learned that it was okay to cry from engaging with my mother and my father, who were both very affectionate and loving "crybabies." There are certain memorable experiences that taught me early in life that it was okay to cry.

My mother and I would watch movies, such as "Imitation of Life," "Native Son," "The Color Purple," and "Steel Magnolias," along with many other tearjerkers, and just cry our eyes out. My dad, on the other hand, loved his music; he loved the blues, and I have developed the same love for it as well.

I recall that my dad and I would sit down and have discussions about how he and my mother met and how they eventually parted ways. He would get so sad at times, he would just cry. He didn't care if I or anyone else saw him or heard him cry—and boy, he would get so loud sometimes.

After a couple of minutes of seeing my dad cry and in so much obvious pain, I would find myself crying with him. Can you envision my 27-year-old dad, sitting beside this then-5-year-old boy, listening to blues recordings, and tears rolling down both our faces? It was too funny!

As my own son was growing up, I have never been ashamed to let him see me cry. I often encouraged him to express his feelings and his emotions; I never told him not to cry and to just be tough. However, I hope I have taught him that *real* men are in tune with their emotions and should never be ashamed to express how they feel— whether it's expressions of love, sadness, disappointment or grief.

I have found that when I am faced with life challenges and when my cup runs over with emotions, and then I cry, it's like taking my soul through the laundromat (as R&B artist Lyfe Jennings wrote in his song "Cry").

It's okay to cry.

In a survey conducted by *Cosmopolitan* (2010), 99% of the women believed that real men do cry, and only 5% of the men said that real men *never* cry— no matter what. The survey also revealed that 39% of the male respondents felt crying was appropriate during tragic moments, and 29% said it was okay for men to cry whenever—just not in public. Interestingly, the remaining 27% felt it was okay for men to get emotional at any time.

Regardless of the statistics and the stigma that is still associated with men who shed a few tears, remember this: If God didn't want us to cry, he would not have designed our bodies to do so. If God has all power in His hand and Jesus still wept, then we must realize that as mortal creatures, we will definitely have our share of rainy days. Why should we feel that men are supposed to be more reserved than God?

My sons, please remember **Psalm 30:5**: "...*[W]eeping may endure for a night, but joy comes in the morning.*" So until everlasting joy comes, it's okay to cry for now.

3

Lessons Learned

It is your God-given right to cry. Don't allow society to reprogram you, shame you or pressure you into suppressing that natural right.

You have a biological need to release your tears. Despite any inner struggle, know that real men and boys *do* cry in response to their feelings.

Real men are in tune with their emotions. Crying should not be something we fight against.

Crying is a healthy way to express emotions. Whether it's during times of happiness, sadness, depression or disappointment, crying is therapeutic and the therapy session is free!

For more guidance, now turn to this Lesson's "Reflections and Resolutions" in the Addendum.

CHAPTER FOUR
Keep Cool. Communicate. Live Violence-Free.

"H.O.P.E. - Hands of Peace & Empathy"
INSPIRED BY: DR. RORY BROWN-SIPP   ILLUSTRATED BY: RICKY SCOTT HOLMES

LIFE LESSON 4
Keep Cool. Communicate. Live Violence-Free.

My sons, this lesson is about the importance of doing your very best to stay calm in stressful and challenging situations. It's also about being mindful of the words you allow to come out of your mouth.

The word of God in **Matthew 15:11** teaches us this: *"It's not what goes in the mouth that defiles the body, but it's what comes out of the mouth that defiles the body."*

This life lesson speaks especially to the importance of keeping your hands to yourself—no hitting, slapping, pushing, or shoving in aggression. It's important to learn the skills that will help you avoid acting out in anger, committing verbal or physical attacks, and disrespecting others.

I particularly want to caution you and help prevent you from ever becoming an abusive perpetrator of domestic violence. You can make better choices.

I'm writing this book to you, my sons, because I am human, and I feel your pain. I have had to deal with some of the same situations and upsets that you are possibly encountering at this time. So I understand. There are times when we all get a little angry. (Forget angry; there are times when I'm simply *mad*.)

Yes, it's okay to feel angry, mad, and even disappointed; these descriptors are natural emotions. But try to understand that it's not so much about feeling those emotions; it's primarily about what we *do* when we are feeling those emotions. Here again, there are choices. I am so grateful that we truly have choices!

My sons, decide which path to walk in your life. There is a crazy path on which you uncontrollably vent your anger, act without thinking, and make any situation worse; or you can follow a different path—a sane one. That's the path on which you keep your cool, step back *mentally*, and assess potentially explosive situations before reacting.

If it ever comes to a moment when you feel you could actually hit someone, immediately step back *physically*, which allows you the time to take a deep breath, let it out slowly, and tell yourself to calm down—even saying it out loud if necessary.

Try to gain a better understanding of the situation; see the role you played in the disagreement and consider the other person's intent regarding his or her actions. **Proverbs 4:7** states, *"…Get wisdom: but in all your getting, get understanding."*

If you realize you have contributed to the situation, acknowledge that, and offer your apologies. Real men own up to their faults and learn from their mistakes.

At times, you will find that your actions were not the primary cause of a disagreement. There will be situations when it's evident that the other person has evil intentions; acknowledge that as well.

It is always a "God thing" to go to any person you had an altercation with and try to work things out civilly, without aggression, when it is possible and safe to do so.

As it says in **Matthew 18:15**, *"If your brother sins, go and show him his fault in private; if he listens to you, you have won your brother."*

Peaceful Communications

My sons, it will benefit you to learn the power of communication, and not just in your personal relationships. Practice communicating openly, honestly, and timely in all aspects of your life. How many lives, relationships, and marriages could have been saved if people simply would have taken the time to talk?

Some people would rather walk around mad at a person for years, not speaking, instead of trying to problem-solve through communication. Some would rather ball up their fists and punch another person, inflicting pain, instead of talking it out. Some would rather grab a gun and end up killing someone's son, daughter, sibling, parent, or spouse instead of talking things through.

In my youth, whenever I had a problem with other kids in the neighborhood, we were told to "talk it out" by the responsible adults. I'm not going to lie; we even had to duke it out (fight) sometimes, but we did not *kill*. And when the disagreement was over, it was over. We did not spend energy feeding and holding on to grudges or trying to retaliate later.

When a person is living his life with integrity and self-respect, he avoids violence and aggression against others. He practices keeping a cool head, keeps his mouth from speaking hurtful words, and keeps his hands to himself even at stressful times of conflict or heated anger.

There probably will be many circumstances in life, my sons, when you will be faced with the need to stay calm and resist striking out verbally or physically at another male or a female.

Domestic Violence and Its Destruction

Of all the forms of violence between people, domestic violence is probably the most prevalent in our society. It occurs regardless of age, race, occupation, socioeconomic status, culture, or nationality. Most often, the victims are women, young children, and teenagers; the perpetrators are most often males.

Domestic violence—aside from the irreversible, permanent tragedy of murder—is the most destructive type of violence and does the longest-lasting emotional damage to survivors and the family circle.

Domestic violence is a general term for any short-term or ongoing violent behavior—whether it's physical assault, verbal abuse, or both—that takes place within a personal relationship and usually starts behind closed doors in the home—the place where every person should feel the safest.

These are some of the abusive behaviors perpetrators use to hurt and control their targets: shoving, punching, slapping, shaking, choking, restraining, verbal put-downs, repeated insults, taunting, scaring, stalking, and isolating victims from their friends and family. In many cases, unwanted sexual advances, forced sexual acts, or sexual assault is inflicted upon the domestic violence victim by the offender—a spouse, someone the victim is dating, or even the person the victim is engaged to marry.

Domestic violence—in any of its varieties—progressively damages victims to their emotional core and can break their spirit. Physical abuse, as well as verbal abuse, gets worse over time. And far too often, my sons, someone ultimately ends up in jail or *dead*.

Statistically, one in every four women in the U.S. will experience domestic violence directly, at some stage of her life. Each year, an estimated 1.3 million women are physically assaulted by an intimate partner, according to the National Coalition Against Domestic Violence.

Although 85 of every 100 domestic violence victims are female, the number of male victims is growing. Regardless of whether the victim or the perpetrator of domestic violence is male or female, married or not, it is *criminal* behavior.

Violence: A Learned Behavior

Based on my personal experience and from my professional perspective, domestic abuse is a *learned* behavior, as are many other violent behaviors. Yes, I say this behavior is learned. As we engage with the world, from infancy to adulthood, we learn a variety of behaviors—both good and bad.

I don't believe that any baby comes from its mother's womb after nine months and enters the world with preformed thoughts or desires to inflict pain upon another human being. Infants are not born with the cognitive abilities or physical capabilities to exhibit aggression or violence towards any other human beings.

Violence is learned through observation and victimization.

In my studies of child development and early childhood education, I learned about philosopher John Locke who believed that children are born "tabula rasa" or as blank slates. Locke said that children's behaviors are formed and changed through their experiences in the world.

To some extent, I believe Locke's viewpoint, but I also believe that elements of our DNA contribute to our inherited temperament, character, and dispositions. (In some cases, genetic disorders or head injuries affecting certain parts of the brain may be contributing to undesirable behaviors.) Wrong behaviors and reactions that are learned, however, can be changed and replaced with new, right-minded, God-directed actions.

Being a man who has dealt with the pain of domestic violence, my experiences could have led me to choose a negative path in life instead of the one I chose. I could have learned the wrong behaviors of domestic violence, fully embraced that violence, and engaged in many awful acts.

But I thank God that wasn't the case. I realized I was free to choose the right path, vowing never to engage in domestic violence or to use physical aggression to solve problems.

When I was a young child and as I grew older, I was surrounded by the effects of domestic violence: anxiety, fear of the unknown, uncertainty, and depression.

Although I don't recall being an eyewitness to any of the physical or verbal abuse inflicted upon my mother, nor did I see firsthand any of those forms of abuse when my sisters and some of my close female friends suffered through it later, I was undoubtedly affected personally by my exposure to domestic violence.

Studies show that children who witness domestic abuse are negatively affected. Many of them, but definitely not all, tend to become abuse victims themselves or act abusively towards others.

Domestic violence creates a cycle that you, my sons, must vow to break wherever it may touch your lives. There is support available for victims, and there are ways to help both youth and adults to end those behaviors.

Empathy And Respect

"Do unto others as you would have them do unto you."

This is known as The Golden Rule, which is expressed in several different ways throughout the Bible and found, in some form, in almost every religion.

Think about how you would feel if someone abused your mother, or your sister, or your little daughter—or even you or another male close to you, because there are men who are victims of domestic violence. You wouldn't appreciate that at all, would you? I know you wouldn't.

When you meet that special young lady, she should become your friend; someone you will respect and trust, and a person you will never feel the desire to harm physically, mentally, or emotionally. (I heard my mother once say, "If her daddy didn't raise her, you definitely can't. So keep your hands to yourself!")

She is a friend, partner, or wife, not a child for you to train. She is not yours to control. The only thing you have control over is yourself—your thoughts, words, and what you do.

It's a sure sign of weakness when a man hits, or in any way abuses, a woman. It truly speaks volumes about his poor character.

To me, it says he is too lazy to problem-solve; he is too lazy— or too lost—to find the requisite words to effectively communicate his thoughts. It says that this man who is engaging in domestic violence is just plain mean! And trust me, my sons, others will think the same thing or even worse. Others will begin to lose respect for him because it will be obvious that he does not respect himself.

A man who respects and loves himself makes certain he maintains a high level of integrity at all times. Integrity means doing the right thing, even when no one sees you or when there is no one present to hold you accountable. Live your life with the highest integrity, and choose to live a God-filled, violence-free life.

My sons, I encourage you to choose this path and pray that you will stay determined to keep your cool and engage in thoughtful, respectful communications with others. Choose to avoid using physical aggression to get your point across or to gain control over your partner or anyone else, in any situation you encounter.

4

Lessons Learned

Choose your own path in life. Regardless of what took place earlier in your life or what types of experiences and exposures to negative influences you endured, you can choose to follow the right path for your life today. Avoid repeating any violent behavior you may have witnessed as a child or young person while growing up.

Stay mindful to keep your anger or temper in check.
No matter what takes place around you, strive to keep your cool. Stay above the arguments and unhealthy communication styles of others who seem to always have lots of drama in their lives.

Keep your hands to yourself, and do not ever take out anger physically on anyone else. It does not matter if it's your partner, spouse, girlfriend, siblings, or someone unrelated to you.

For more guidance, now turn to this Lesson's "Reflections and Resolutions" in the Addendum.

5

CHAPTER FIVE
Abstinence, Intimacy, and Avoiding "Baby Mama" Drama

"Intimacy"
INSPIRED BY: DR. RORY BROWN-SIPP   ILLUSTRATED BY: RICKY SCOTT HOLMES

LIFE LESSON 5
Abstinence, Intimacy, and Avoiding "Baby Mama" Drama

Well, my sons, this is where I bring up the big discussion about "the birds and the bees." This chapter is about choosing abstinence, developing and maintaining appropriate relationships, and understanding the risks of becoming a father too soon.

Discussing topics of this nature is often difficult for parents, yet I can imagine it may be even more difficult for you on the receiving end. Often, parents simply lack any frame of reference for holding this type of conversation with their children because many parents did not experience similar conversations with their own parents, but this *is* a discussion worth having.

Parents may fear having this discussion. Why? They may worry over these two questions: "Will talking about sex influence my child to engage in sexual activity?" and "Will having this discussion send a message that I support my child's engaging in sexual activity?"

Parents' own doubts and fears are often the cause of their wrong thinking, resulting in "putting it off until later" or "just skipping it altogether," which means they avoid this highly important but delicate—maybe even uncomfortable—conversation about abstinence, relationships, and avoiding premature parenting. And too often that is the very thing that contributes to early teen sexual activity, sexually transmitted diseases (STDs), and teenage pregnancy, now almost epidemic in our communities.

Recent statistics regarding sexual activity among teens in the United States show that the percentage of high school students who are having sex differs significantly by race and ethnicity, according to the National Campaign to Prevent Teen and Unplanned Pregnancy. Premature sexual activity of high school students was reportedly most prevalent among Black students, at 60%; the percentages for Hispanics/Latinos and Caucasians were somewhat lower at 49% and 44% respectively.

Furthermore, there are other ramifications of engaging in premature sex about which teens are usually uneducated and unprepared. One in four Human Immunodeficiency Virus (HIV) infections in the U.S. occurred in youth between the ages of 13 and 24, but occurrence rates were higher for Black males than any other group, according to the Center for Disease Control and Prevention (CDC). It was also noted that 60% of all youth with HIV, regardless of their race or ethnicity, (1) did not know they were infected, (2) were not getting treatment, and (3) unknowingly passed the virus on to others. The CDC further noted there were approximately 117 *teenage* pregnancies per 1,000 total pregnancies (whether terminated early or carried to full term).

The statistics are depressing. What's even more disconcerting to me personally is that I can't recall my school providing a sex education course in high school regarding abstinence, safe sex, STDs—or anything of the sort.

Thinking back, I can't recall ever having a sit-down conversation about sexual behavior with either of my parents, my grandparents, or my older siblings. I'd have to say that I don't think I received *any* guidance. (Oh yes… my grandmother did have just *one* sit-down session with me when I inquired about sex. The 'conversation' was short, sweet, and to the point. She simply said to me, in her stern, Southern voice, "Don't even *think* about having sex! Go *sit down* somewhere!")

Since my grandmother probably never had a conversation with her parents or grandparents regarding sex, she didn't realize that she was missing a teachable moment with me. She could have explained the importance of abstinence, developing appropriate relationships, choosing healthy companions, safe sex, and responsible parenting. She had to have known I would meet someone special one day, someone with whom I would want to develop a close relationship, and intimacy would then follow.

Okay, that's enough talk about the problem of who didn't receive guidance from whom way back when. I want to be a part of the solution *today* by providing you, my sons, with insight regarding the decisions and choices you young men ought to make as you naturally move in the direction toward sexual desire and intimacy.

When my biological son was very young, I made a vow that I wouldn't avoid having difficult conversations with him—conversations that would assist him on his life's journey and conversations that would offer information about sexual activity.

Our first talks were simply about helping him identify and understand his anatomy. I wanted him not only to understand the functions of his body but also to know the correct terminology when talking about his body parts. I wanted him to be aware of the fact that he is a male and to articulate that he has a penis. No euphemisms or baby-talk terms were acceptable.

Next, I wanted him to know that no one other than his mother or I should touch his genitals or any other private body part, except for a medical professional or an authorized family member—even then, touching must be for appropriate purposes. I talked to him about appropriate touching as opposed to inappropriate touching.

Children can usually tell when a situation doesn't feel quite right to them, and they should be encouraged to speak up. It's never too early to start sex education, as long as the child's age and developmental level is taken into consideration.

As my son grew older, I wanted to make certain he understood the importance of abstinence. I had that discussion with him at 8 or 9 years of age. Some may consider that too young an age at which to start such a conversation, but it's probably not.

About Abstinence

According to the CDC, teens are reportedly having their first sexual activity, including intercourse, as early as age 13. The CDC reports statistics on teenagers who even contracted HIV or AIDS, tragically, while in that same age group or younger.

I wanted my son to understand that sex is an activity that should take place between responsible, consenting adults only—not between children. I wanted him to know it is a natural act, an act that ought to be between adults expressing love and passion for one another (the operative word being *adults*).

My sons, if you are not considered an adult, and if you are not at least 18 years of age, you should refrain from having any form of sexual activity with anyone. I would be a hypocrite if I were to tell you not to try developing a relationship with someone to whom you feel attracted. Also, I would be lying if I were to say I was not intimate and sexually active as a teenager. But I would be remiss if I didn't tell you it was reckless and risky.

Naturally, your body will begin to have normal urges for sex, but you have to beat down the desires of your flesh! This means, as Apostle Paul in **1 Corinthians 9:27** states: *"I discipline my body like an athlete, training it to do what it should. Otherwise, I fear that after preaching to others I myself might be disqualified."*

Candidly, I am warning you how the flesh will naturally yearn for and want to yield to tempestuous and sexual activities, but the word and spirit of God demands that we obey His commandments and *wait*.

Instead of focusing on sex during your childhood and teen years, it is smarter for you to concentrate on your future as you learn how to enjoy life respectfully and responsibly. It is your responsibility to get your education by staying in school, studying, and focusing on graduating in order for you to become a positive, contributing citizen in our society.

Enjoy life, but burn off some of the tension. Occupy your mind by getting involved in extracurricular activities at school, in the community, and at church. Try out for the basketball or football team. Run track. Play an instrument in the marching or concert band. Volunteer in the community and assist other young men. Volunteer your time at your local Boys and Girls Club. Become a member of Big Brothers, Big Sisters, a mentoring program, or become active doing service in your church.

You can attend youth nights where you interact with other young men and women of God. You can serve with the outreach ministry and go out into your local community to tell others about the word of God. There are so many things you can choose to take part in as a young person. Doing positive activities will keep you busy and help to keep your mind off sex.

The time will come when it's appropriate for you to have sexual relationships. Trust me. As my son transitioned into the latter part of his teenage years and as he approached the age of maturity, our talks regarding abstinence, intimacy, and companionship evolved into in-depth conversations regarding responsible parenting and safe sex. I explained to him that the safest form of protection is abstinence. Of course, I realized that he (a young, good-looking male) would not abstain forever.

Truly, the word of God wants us to procreate. **Genesis 1:28** states: *"God blessed them and said to them, be fruitful and increase in number; fill the earth and subdue it. Rule over the fish in the sea and the birds in the sky and over every living creature that moves on the ground."* But I want to make certain there are no confusions here, so I direct you to read what it states in **1 Corinthians, Chapter 7**: *"But because of the temptation to sexual immorality, each man should have his own wife and each woman her own husband."*

Since my son wasn't married, and after I realized that abstinence was out of the question, I tried to put the fear of God in him, while at the same time educating him regarding the effects of sexually transmitted diseases. I gave him graphic details on what he could anticipate if he engaged in unprotected sexual activity. I explained to him how to protect himself. And I didn't mean protected only in the sense of ensuring he wears a condom each time, but *protected* in the sense of taking time to learn more about his sexual partner *before* jumping in the bed together.

Just as I told my biological son, I will say the same thing to each of my sons who are reading this: Plain and simple, "Have sex with your wife—not with a 'baby mama.'" First and foremost, don't have sex out of wedlock. Get married first, and then enjoy the pleasures of your marriage. I'm realistic, so I understand that not everyone will wait, get married first, and then be sexually active. As I stated to my son, "Have sex with your wife," or at least preserve yourself for someone with whom you anticipate spending the rest of your life.

After I first said that to him, he looked at me as if I had gone crazy! He didn't understand the message I was trying to convey to him. My message then, which I repeat today for all of my sons, is good advice: "Get to know the young lady first."

Seek to understand more about her mindset, her temperament, and her lifestyle; determine if she loves and respects herself. Ask her about her dreams and aspirations in life to see if this is the person you want to share your entire life with—or at least any significant part of it.

Be sure that she loves the same God you love. Ask God, ask yourself, and ask the responsible adult who serves as a mother-figure to you, "Is this young lady my wife?" (You know you have to get your mother's approval whenever possible.) If the answer is yes, marry her; continue to invest in your friendship, enjoy intimacy, and then be sexual in your marriage.

Keep this in mind: Intimacy is not necessarily the same thing as having sex. Intimacy can be defined as a close, familiar, and usually affectionate, loving interpersonal relationship with another person. My description of intimacy encompasses holding hands, hugging, sharing a movie or a special moment together; it may even be having one small, quick kiss. (Well, okay, a *big* kiss—but nothing more!)

Oftentimes, young men fail to take precautions. Many will foolishly let their eyes and lustful ways dictate to them, driving them into multiple sexual relationships. Not only is that self-disrespect, it's a way of selling yourself cheaply. It is also a setup for a lot of financial and mental anguish. When young people do not practice safe sex—even one time—they can catch a sexually transmitted disease. That can cost a lot: money for medical treatment, of course; however, sometimes the price is higher—death from a disease.

Whenever you get involved with multiple sex partners, with any woman who is not your wife (and not even a good prospect to be your wife), you put yourself at risk for fathering children by these women, each of whom you would shamefully refer to as "my baby mama."

Then comes the "baby mama" drama…

The drama comes in the form of the mothers fighting with one another, verbally or physically, because there is conflict when there are multiple women, all of their children, yet only one man. The drama then continues when, as happens quite often, the court is invited in or forced into the situation.

Next, there are trial dates, fees and legal expenses, paternity tests, loss of parental rights or limited child visitation, and court-ordered child support payments. When fees are not paid, get ready to have driving privileges revoked, other licenses blocked, wage garnishments, and possibly worse—jail time.

I could write an entire book on baby-mama-type drama just based on horror stories I've heard from others. You've probably heard some too, right?

In my case, I escaped that type of problem. Although my son's mother and I didn't marry, she was an excellent candidate for becoming my wife.

To this date, I thank God there never was any baby-mama-drama trauma.
(Thank you, Leslie.)

I am not making light of this destructive drama, nor am I diminishing the seriousness of such dysfunctional behavior and its long-term negative impact on the children. I am pointing out to you, my sons, the messy and unhappy consequences of being negligent and having unprotected sex with multiple partners—or even one partner— if that results in pregnancy.

My sons, I want to help you make better choices in your youth. Use good judgment and follow God's word to help you stay abstinent in order to stay free from drama and disease. By doing so, you can lead productive, sexually healthy lives as adults.

5

Lessons Learned

Enjoy life. There is a lot more to life than sex. You can redirect some of the natural energy and keep sex off your mind by occupying it with other activities, such as getting involved in community events, joining youth groups at church, and doing extracurricular sports at school.

Stay focused. While you are young, focus on what's most important: stay in school, get a good education, and make positive contributions to society.

Practice self-control. Having sex too soon, when you are ill-prepared and unprotected, not only compromises your youthful years, it also puts you at risk for sexually transmitted diseases that could lead to your death.

Understand your body. Know the names for your body parts and understand how they work—internally and externally.

Be patient. You can enjoy intimacy in your loving relationships without sex. The time will come when it's appropriate to have sexual relationships, but until the time is right, be patient… and wait.

For more guidance, now turn to this Lesson's "Reflections and Resolutions" in the Addendum.

CHAPTER SIX
Education, Enterprise, and Empowerment

"Two Roads, One Dream"
INSPIRED BY: DR. RORY BROWN-SIPP   ILLUSTRATED BY: RICKY SCOTT HOLMES

LIFE LESSON 6
Education, Enterprise, and Empowerment

The goal of this lesson is to point out some truths about getting your education, choosing an income-generating enterprise, and becoming empowered in all areas of your life.

My sons, you will read about FAPE laws and why none of us in America ought to take our education for granted. I will offer you a tool—PAID—that will help you learn and earn, grow and prosper, and develop greater self-respect and success in your life.

My sons, I am hopeful you will receive a jolt of energy and feel inspired to continue your education, value holding a job, enter a promising career, start a business, or consider whether enlisting in the military is an option for you. If for some reason you have stopped going to school or have quit working, I believe this lesson will motivate you to continue your education and pursue a job or career so you will feel a sense of dignity and earn the respect of others.

EDUCATION

First, understand your responsibilities for your own education; second, know that you have legal rights protecting you from being denied an education.

Unlike in our nation's past, you now have vast opportunities for getting schooling. Learn how that came about, understand the significance, and uphold your duty to respect and honor the men, women, and youth who struggled, sacrificed, shed blood, and even suffered death to ensure those rights for all of us.

Before many of you came into this world, and even before I was born, the path had already been made and a foundation was laid whereby we would have freedom, equality, and access. Not only are we free to attend educational institutions today, but we have legally protected rights to countless other necessary or desirable services and facilities.

I particularly want to emphasize the value of an academic education, my sons, because that—to get a basic education in this country—is one of your civil rights. Under the law, you are entitled to a "free, appropriate, public education" or FAPE, regardless of any barriers such as learning challenges, mobility needs, mental or physical impairment, socioeconomic status, developmental difficulties, or other disadvantages.

Whether you are merely curious or planning to pursue a career such as mine in education and child development or a related field, it's interesting to study the advancements made to our country's educational system, which started in the 1840s—when education went from being strictly private to first becoming available publicly—and on through the late 1950s when the government started providing federal funding for education.

Beyond that, a long progression of laws and mandates—with acronyms such as IDEA, ESEA, IEPs, and LREs, and various so-called acts and titles—expanded the protection for students regardless of color, gender, economic level, or physical and mental ability. Today, my sons, all of you benefit—but always remember what a tremendous amount of time and human effort those safeguards took before they became the law.

Education rights are based upon the principles of civil rights.

No matter what your ethnicity or ability, the right to education, especially for Blacks, was solidly secured during the early Civil Rights Movement and later through court cases such as Brown v. Board of Education. Those rights remain in place thanks to education advocates who continue to make sure there is legal access to education for all children.

Many young men and women have dedicated their lives to fighting for civil rights, for all people to be treated equally. Some of them who were martyrs in the fight for rights for Black Americans in particular are highlighted in this lesson. For certain, there were others of every race who fought as well, and I am grateful for all of them, pay tribute to them, and say that we must learn more about their contributions, which helped shape and transform our educational system into what it is today.

Generally when we speak about civil rights, we commonly refer to the rights that prohibit racial or gender discrimination in voting, housing, hiring, and so forth. And while they were huge gains, I want to call attention to the civil rights in the area of education.

Laws that entitle all Americans to a free and appropriate public education are among the most important civil rights we have. Please, my sons, do not take this freedom for granted or take it lightly! That right was secured for all of us by people who came before us and made civil rights a reality; some paid with their lives, and others suffered horrible fates, but they would not turn back from fighting for that justice.

Among them were teenagers and young men—kind of like you, my sons—who paid the ultimate price. Read about three of them—Chaney, Goodman, and Schwerner—in the Lessons Learned section at the end of this chapter. Others were older and wiser with a lot to lose: they were parents with infants and young children, small business merchants and farmers, and clergy members such as the most well-known civil rights leader, Rev. Martin Luther King, Jr.

In case no one ever told you about your right to pursue an education, let me share some things with you from our nation's history and from what I learned in my youth as a student attending school in the Deep South.

Growing up in Birmingham, Alabama in the early 1970s, not too far removed from all of the overt oppression, degradation, and segregation of the Deep South, I did not realize how newly privileged I was as a Black child to be afforded the opportunity to attend school alongside my White classmates. I thought school had always been open to everyone.

Back then, I was oblivious to the struggles which had taken place over the 200 years prior to my birth and was too young to fully understand the escalating struggles for civil rights in the decades leading up to the 1970s. Those hard fought battles resulted in free, appropriate, public education and, eventually, racially integrated schools in America.

I had no idea that the educational freedoms and opportunities I had for a good education were completely denied to my parents, my grandparents, and my great grandparents. Thinking back, I used to imagine what types of classes my parents and grandparents might have taken compared to mine. I knew that my generation had far better technology and tools in our schools than they could have had. Of course my immediate ancestors probably sat in a classroom the same way I did along with my peers—or so I thought. I recall how I was beyond disbelief when I realized none of my ancestors received any form of formal education at all!

Worse yet, in those days they were forbidden from even attempting to educate themselves after being forced onto slave ships and brought to the shores of this continent long before it became the United States of America. I understood in part how my ancestors were deprived of their God-given right to freedom and were made to work as slaves, cultivating the land and cotton fields, providing uncompensated industrial labor to the slaveholders.

But worst of all, there was such a prohibition against early African-American Blacks being educated that laws were soon established in support of the colonies and states which denied slaves the opportunity to even read and write. Slave owners feared that if slaves ever became educated—or at least learned to read and write—they would become informed, enlightened, and self-determined, then likely develop aspirations to escape plantations or engage in rebellions against their so-called masters.

Many Black ancestors were hung simply for looking at a book or trying to read one.

The practice of mistreating Black people and depriving them of learning to read and write or even having a basic educational experience would continue for many years, long after legalized slavery ended and Blacks had been granted their first steps toward freedom.

In my opinion, Blacks were merely transitioned from one system of slavery to being enslaved by yet another: They still were not granted human rights, especially freedoms that pertained to education and access to public facilities.

According to **Galatians 5:1**, *"It is for freedom that Christ has set us free. Stand firm, then, and do not let yourselves be burdened again by a yoke of slavery."* When I became an adult, I learned more about the long struggle and the ongoing fight for educational equality and integration for Black Americans.

Most of us who were born in the 1970s heard about Dr. King most of our lives. He had a faith and hope that race-based bigotry would end, and he actively worked toward that goal. But did you know that as a direct result of his efforts—and the work of other legendary and some not-so-well-known activists of the early Civil Rights Movement—our modern-day rights to receive a quality public education were cemented into our country's laws?

Nearly all of the landmark victories guaranteeing equality in school facilities for all students of color, as well as students with physical and other challenges, were enacted during that time. The civil rights struggle was in great part responsible for the most significant strides made in the U.S. educational system.

Your right to a free and fair education is *your* civil right. Remember that, my sons, and appreciate the role your education plays in improving your chances for better work, better pay, and making your life better in other ways.

ENTERPRISE

My sons, I want to help you understand why it is important to *prepare* for success in any lawful line of work and avoid the illegal types of enterprises that will surely tear you down, limit your options, and kill our communities, or possibly take your own life away too soon—no matter how much money it may generate for a while… until something goes terribly wrong for you or others.

Be enterprising and use your skills and brains to make an honest income. No honest job is too small or insignificant; it is good and proper to work for a living.

No matter what course of study or which type of income source you choose, I just want you to become actively involved in something positive and constructive. It is never too late to make a decision to get on and stay on the road to a better future.

For some strange reason, a lot of young men today have every excuse in the book for why they can't go to work. My sons, if you have ever said anything similar to, "I don't want to work at any fast food place," or "I don't want to work at any grocery market," or "I'm not going to be a box clerk at a discount chain store," or something like that, the only thing people really hear you saying is, "I DON'T WANT TO WORK!"

Here's what you ought to be saying instead: "I will flip burgers until I become a barber," or "I will bag groceries for shoppers until I can buy my own auto repair shop," or "I will stock shelves at the local Walmart on my way to becoming a stockbroker on Wall Street."

If you imagine yourself becoming mayor someday, there is nothing wrong with learning how to manage time, money, and people by working at McDonald's first. You could even choose to move up the corporate ladder from a janitor to a manager. Do you get the point?

Whether you earn $7.25 an hour or $70,000 a year, appreciate whatever work you can find and do it responsibly. Don't feel embarrassed to work in any honest job when you need to earn money, and be grateful to have any work at all.

I'm not telling you to do anything I haven't done already and continue to do each and every day of my life. I started working when I was 14 years old. It wasn't because I had to, I just wanted to make my own money and pay my own way. It took some of the load off of my parents when I could buy some of the things I wanted and contribute to the household finances.

I have worked more types of jobs than you might imagine. Before becoming a professional executive in the field of education, I worked at Burger King, Winn Dixie grocery, several department stores, and did jobs for telecommunication offices; and the list goes on. I worked both through high school and while I was getting my college degrees.

Making a decent living is far better than living dangerously by selling drugs, pimping, stealing, robbing, and cheating. Living a life of crime is not a career, it's just *that*—a life of crime!

My sons, your self-respect and self-esteem will be raised when you are righteously earning your way in this world and not being dependent upon others to pay your way. Even God, who loves us dearly, commands us to work. **John 9:4** states: "*We must quickly carry out the tasks assigned us by the one who sent us. The night is coming, and then no one can work.*"

Further, **2 Thessalonians 3:10** states: "*For even when we were with you, we gave you this rule: The one who is unwilling to work shall not eat.*"

EMPOWERMENT

One of the best ways to empower yourself in this society is to get a good education, make respectable choices regarding your source of income, and be a responsible man who provides service to his community and country. Today, a young man can be just about anything he decides he wants to be.

When I was in elementary school during the late '70s, our teachers would sometimes ask us what we wanted to become when we grew up. Many of us named jobs such as "police officer," "teacher," or "nurse."

I don't recall hearing any of my peers ever saying, "I want to grow up to be the president of the United States," or "I will run for mayor of my city," or "I'll get elected governor of my state." I don't recall anyone ever saying, "I will be a scientist," or "I want to be an architect."

In those days, we did not look any further than the options our parents were limited to because of racial segregation and other roadblocks imposed upon them and their ancestors. So we just assumed none of us would ever be able to hold prominent political positions or work in jobs and professions that were generally off limits for Black Americans. I can tell you that the idea of an African-American man becoming the president of the United States was unimaginable and unachievable—until now.

On Nov 11, 2008, and again four years later, President Barack Obama proved that a young man could become whatever he decides to become—even this country's president. He did it in what I refer to as the PAID way—by *persevering*, utilizing *access* to education, and *investing* time and energy wisely, with a serious *dedication* to succeed.

Today, we hear young men on the streets boasting, "I'm gonna get *paid*."

But are they really?

Are they aware and ready to do what's healthy and right?

If so, what system will they use to reach success?

Using the PAID Life System

PAID is a tool I believe you can use throughout your life, my sons, to ensure you will be in a better position to earn what you want, doing the work you prefer, and reaching other goals you want for yourself, but only after you learn what it takes. PAID can be applied to all areas of your life, and I'll share with you how to use this tool. Basically, it amounts to making these four action concepts a habit:

Perseverance: Stick to your plans and don't give up when you want to achieve something positive for yourself and your family. Work hard and stay on the right track. You will have the victory if you persevere.

Access: You have rights—to education, to work, to vote, to serve your country, just to name a few. So know what they are and use them wisely and responsibly. No one is going to hand anything to you on a silver platter; you have to access it by going where you need to go, doing what is required, preparing yourself, and then you can get the benefits and rewards of having access and choices.

Investment (Time and Energy): This action is critical because all you have to work with is time and energy in order to do anything in life. Your time must be invested wisely in school and in doing work that advances you toward something positive. Don't waste your time or your energy doing negative and foolish things or hanging around with negative people in your life, because that will bring you down or lead to trouble, jail or death.

Dedication: Are you really committed and working toward what you say you want? Being dedicated means you are willing to take the proper steps and do the work necessary—without excuses. Be deliberate, stay focused, and stick to the course of action you need to take.

It is important to understand that you can decide whether to live your life well or waste it. Most definitely, my sons, don't let anyone convince you that crime will pay off for you or get you any real power.

If you choose the low-life path to what seems like easy (but illegal) money, you are choosing a weak, deadly pathway. Instead of traveling down or staying on that dead end road, try empowering yourself, investing your time and energy to become something more.

Empowerment is not all about the money.

Empowerment is about you and what you hope to achieve in your life.

By now, I hope you can see clearly how insulting and disheartening it is to parents, grandparents, and the many other elders who struggled so hard—risking their lives to make things better for future generations—when they see how many young people today don't understand or even care about their rights and responsibilities.

When our elders see how some young people refuse to be responsible—refusing to work, refusing to go to school, refusing to vote, and even refusing to pull up their sagging pants—it must be heartbreaking for them, and it is totally disrespectful to them.

I didn't write this chapter to enrage you, my sons. I wrote it to empower you to get up and get busy! There are no more excuses. You have access to schools and jobs, and you can aim for the career of your choice.

You can use all of your time, energy, and freedom—now that you have it—to be even more dedicated and willing to persevere as other young men have done in the past. Be sure to take time to read this chapter's Lessons From History and the brief stories about the young freedom fighters and be inspired by their stories.

When you empower yourself, you determine your future by moving in the direction of earning a living, building a life of purpose, and fulfilling your duty to be of service to your family community, while first giving thanks to God for all your blessings.

6

Lessons Learned

Use the PAID life system. It stands for perseverance, access, investment of time and energy, and dedication. Make these things a habit and become empowered to improve any area of your life.

Be willing to do other types of work until you can secure that dream job, career, or business. Avoid being too selective about where you will and will not work. Any legal, ethical job can be a good one for now.

Know your civil rights and capitalize on your freedom. In the USA, you are free to get an education, work, vote, travel, and serve your country. Appreciate it and take advantage of these invaluable opportunities.

Honor those who fought for civil rights. The rights you enjoy today were paid for by others who fought long and hard to get and keep them. Use your voting power, speak up for justice, and recognize your duty to uphold those rights. Remember the lessons from the past to make a better future for yourself and your descendants.

For more guidance, now turn to this Lesson's "Reflections and Resolutions" in the Addendum.

6

LESSONS FROM HISTORY
Honoring Civil Rights Pioneers

There are too many to name in this section, but here we pay honor to some of the individuals who gave their lives to make it possible for Black Americans and other historically disadvantaged groups to have an equal opportunity and to gain fair access in all areas of life.

Today, we have the freedom to choose where we want to live, where we'd like to attend school, which jobs or professions we'd like to pursue, and whether to run for political office; we are free to make other choices we ought never to take for granted. Each of us must do our part to keep those freedoms.

Countless civil rights fighters were young people. Many of them were only adolescents or teenagers when they took part in dangerous protests or marches to stand up against a powerful system of racism and other forms of bigotry.

As you read about these legends—the young and the elderly—try to imagine the repeated brutality they faced in the fight, which was often to the death, and remeber that your freedom to live, learn, and earn were bought by their bold, courageous actions and their bloodshed.

Medgar Wiley Evers *was a Black American activist who worked as a field secretary for the National Association for the Advancement of Colored People (NAACP). He lived in Mississippi and fought tirelessly for civil rights and equality, and he fought against segregation. He was murdered on June 12, 1963 by Byron De La Beckwith, a member of the White Citizens Council, in the front yard of the Evers family homes while his wife and young children slept inside.*

James Earl Chaney, *only 21 years old at the time of his death, was a young Black American from Meridian, Mississippi;* **Andrew Goodman**, *who was 20 years old at the time of his death, was a Jewish civil rights activist from New York; and* **Michael "Mickey" Schwerner**, *who was 25 years old at the time of his death, was also a Jewish civil rights worker from New York.*

All three were members of the Congress of Racial Equality (CORE) and worked together in support of Blacks in Mississippi who were fighting for equal opportunity, integration in public places, equal employment opportunities, and the right to vote. Unfortunately, their fight for civil rights ended prematurely when all three young men were abducted, beaten, shot, hung, and then buried by members of the Mississippi White Knights of the Ku Klux Klan.

Their murders occurred on June 21, 1964. The FBI referred to the crime investigation as Mississippi Burning or MIBURN.

After the largest and most televised search of that time, the civil rights workers' bodies were found 44 days later in an earthen dam—a high pile of dirt—near the murder site. The murders of these three young men sparked national outrage and served as the catalyst for the signing of the Civil Rights Act of 1964 and the Voting Rights Act of 1965.

Rev. Dr. Martin Luther King, Jr., *from Atlanta, Georgia, was an activist, a clergyman, the leader of the Montgomery Bus Boycott, and an organizer of the most well-known, non-violent protests against segregation in the Southern states, particularly in Alabama and Georgia.*

Dr. King led peaceful protests in support of equal civil rights for all citizens; he instructed participants on non-violent protest methods and civil disobedience for positive social change.

He led the great March on Washington for Jobs and Freedom on August 28, 1963, where he delivered a multifaceted speech—"I Have a Dream"—which addressed ending racial segregation, but it also carried a strong message calling for economic empowerment for the poor and an end to poverty, especially for historically disadvantaged people of color.

In 1964, he became the youngest person to be awarded a Nobel Peace Prize.

He was assassinated by James Earl Ray who shot him on April 4, 1968.

CHAPTER SEVEN
The Gift of Christ

"The Gift"
INSPIRED BY: DR. RORY BROWN-SIPP   ILLUSTRATED BY: RICKY SCOTT HOLMES

LIFE LESSON 7
The Gift of Christ

Over the years, and especially since my son's birth, I have been big on giving. I love giving gifts and I love occasions that allow me the opportunity to give to others. I particularly love birthdays and graduations, and I am most fond of Christmas. I love the whole spirit and feeling of the holiday season, the loving care shown to one another, and the giving of gifts in all forms. I guess it is an attribute of my culture and my experiences as a child that make me enjoy giving so much.

When I was young, my family made a concerted effort to ensure that they gave my siblings and me everything we needed and some of those special items we *wanted*, as well. I can recall the annual birthday parties, the festive Christmas celebrations, and the proud graduation ceremonies, all of which were accompanied by happy gift-giving.

I was in my late teenage years—after I had become a parent and after my grandparents and mother had all passed away—when I realized I had been given one very special, life-giving gift. It was *that* family treasure which had been passed down from generation to generation. It was *that* gift which my grandparents and parents had given me so long ago. It was and is the gift of *Christ*.

It wasn't until I had gone through many adversities and had fallen down several times—yet mysteriously continued to get back up, even when I thought I wanted to die—*that* I realized it wasn't my holding on for survival that kept me alive, it was *God* holding on to me. It was that gift of Christ in my heart which keeps on giving and has sustained me as it continues to protect me to this day.

When I was younger—definitely prior to developing my own personal relationship with Christ—I did not understand the hype about getting up every Sunday around 6 a.m. to be in church for Sunday school that started at 10 a.m., especially since actual morning services didn't start until 11 a.m. and ended around 1 or 2 p.m. That was four hours of church; half of a work shift; one-sixth of an entire day! I did not get it!

Well, my sons, if you are presented with the opportunity to fully engage in spiritual or church activities, or if you are currently engaged in such, please hear me loud and clear: Spending all the time and effort is worth it! It is through participation in church that you can experience your gift. It is in Sunday school, church services, and evening Bible studies that you will get to understand more about the gift of Christ; all the while, you will be developing your own personal relationship with him.

I was so accustomed to looking at *materialistic* gifts that I almost overlooked my *spiritual* gift. As I became wiser as a man and a Christian father, I realized my son needed to get a gift he could own and cherish forever, a gift that could not be replaced with a newer prototype the following year. In addition to all of the electronic game systems, $200-a-pair gym shoes, and name-brand clothing, my son needed to receive a gift that wouldn't diminish in value after being used a few times. I had to make sure he got a permanent gift that would *never* go out of style.

I will not be here for my son forever, nor will I be able to write self-help guides, such as this one, forever, but I knew I could leave something for him that will last long after I've gone away. The eternal *gift of Christ* is the best gift I could ever give to anyone, including to you, my sons.

When my son was very young, I introduced him to Jesus by talking about his goodness. I exposed my son to the teachings of Jesus by taking him with me to attend church every Sunday. I wanted him to witness me and other Christians praying, praising and worshiping Jesus. I even wanted him to see God's people moving and operating under the anointing.

My hope was that someday my son would receive and experience the same anointing and presence of God for himself. When my son began to read as he grew older, I got him his own personal Bible and directed him to certain scriptural passages and pointed out the important lessons to be learned.

In introducing Christ to you, my sons—just as I introduced my son, Reshaude, to Him many years ago—the first thing I want you to know is that Jesus Christ is real and alive, dwelling within us all, each and every day. Secondly, you will need to have your own personal Bible as well. Get a Bible you like; ideally, choose one that is accessible and easy to carry around with you, such as a digital download you can carry on your cell phone or iPad. Select the version that is easiest for you to read and understand.

Pray before reading the Bible. Study to "show thyself approved unto God" as **2 Timothy 2:15** directs us. Then pray after you have finished reading. Use your Bible as one of your many road maps in life. Guidance on any topic can be found in the Bible.

"*What has been will be again; what has been done will be done again: there is nothing new under the sun,*" it states in **Ecclesiastes 1:9**. There is guidance on topics such as crime, killing, sex, sexuality, greed, overspending… you name it and it's there. Honoring the physical body is one of the major topics critical for all of us, but it is especially important for young people who are learning about self-care and how to stay healthy. It is sometimes a matter of life and death when the body is mistreated. Here again, the Bible is a great source of instruction.

Remember this: Your body is your temple; take good care of it—you only get one. It is vital for you, my sons, to stay toxin-free to the best of your ability. I encourage you to stay away from illegal drugs and to avoid using other harmful substances, but I must also mention another popular practice to avoid—*tattoos*—because that would also compromise your temple.

I admit that I have three tattoos, but I got them when I was much younger and did not know any better. It took one of my family members to teach me a much-needed lesson. (Surprisingly, it was one who no one would have assumed could give out much good advice since he was intoxicated most of the time.) When he saw I had been tattooed, he directed me to the word of God in **Leviticus 19:28**: *"Ye shall not make any cuttings in your flesh for the dead, nor print or tattoo any marks upon you: I am the Lord."*

I then found another scripture that spoke about protecting your body—the temple. **1 Corinthians 6:19-20** reads: *"What? Know ye not that your body is the temple of the Holy Ghost which is in you, which ye have of God, and ye are not your own? For ye are bought with a price: therefore glorify God in your body, and in your spirit, which are God's."*

In addition, another noteworthy topic the Bible instructs you about, my sons, is how to regard your parents, as we read in **Ephesians 6:2**: *"Honor your father and your mother—which is the first commandment with a promise."*

Further, **Deuteronomy 5:16** states: *"Honor your father and your mother, as the Lord God has commanded you so that you may live long and that it may go well with you in the land the Lord your God is giving you."*

Not only did God give us the gift of Jesus Christ, Christ gave us our parents as gifts we should always cherish. He left us specific instructions on this topic, and so many others, to make certain we would remain in compliance.

I leave you with the scriptures I referenced, which are some of the Bible lessons I've shared with my son. But most of all, I leave you with the most wonderful gift—*Christ!*

The Lord's Prayer

This, then, is how you should pray:

Our Father in heaven, hallowed be your name.

Your kingdom come, your will be done, on earth as it is in heaven.

Give us today our daily bread.

And forgive us our debts, as we also have forgiven our debtors.

And lead us not into temptation, but deliver us from the evil one,

for yours is the kingdom and the power and the glory, forever.

Amen.

7

Lessons Learned

Read your Bible or your spiritual guide as one of your many road maps to life. Guidance on nearly any subject can be found in the Bible. Read it regularly.

Respect your body and take good care of it, for it is your temple. Commune with God both day and night. Your strength comes from the Lord. Receive and hold on to the gift of Christ with all your heart.

Pray daily day and night. In the mornings, give thanks unto the Lord for giving you one more chance to get it right. Adopt a prayer to say every night. Pray anytime, in any situation. On the opposite page is The Lord's Prayer which comes from **Matthew 6:9-13**.

For more guidance, now turn to this Lesson's "Reflections and Resolutions" in the Addendum.

ADDENDUM

A Psalm to My Sons
7 Easy Life Lessons and Spiritual Guidance
Written by Dr. Rory Brown-Sipp

Reflections & Resolutions

This *Reflections and Resolutions* worksheet section is a place for readers to review and write about each of the author's seven chapters, or Life Lessons. This section can be useful whether the book is being used as a self-help guide by an individual, in an instructor-led classroom, or in a youth group setting.

It may be most helpful to complete the *Reflections and Resolutions* questions for each chapter immediately after reading it. This guided supplement helps reinforce the corresponding Life Lesson in each chapter and the Lessons Learned summary content which follows each chapter.

Suggestion for using Reflections: This section gives readers a chance to think over the specific concepts in the respective chapter and to see how they may apply to his life. The questions help guide the thought and discussion process.

Suggestion for using Resolutions: Readers may use this section primarily to write goals and plans for growth and development related to that chapter's topic and key points. Use this section to make commitments, plan next steps, and set goals to work toward success.

Reflections & Resolutions
"A Psalm to My Sons" by Dr. Rory Brown-Sipp

Life Lesson 1

Son, Father, Man, Christian, Leader

Reflections

1.1 What initial thoughts did you have as you were reading this chapter?

___

1.2 Which parts of this chapter's Life Lesson are the most significant to you? Which points are most useful for you? Why?

___

1.3 Have you ever experienced anything similar to what you've read about in this chapter?

___

1.4 Is someone close to you going through anything similar to what you've read in this chapter? If so, has this Life Lesson helped you understand that person's situation better? Do you believe you are likely to share any part of this Life Lesson with another person?

___

1.5 Are you currently feeling like you are a "real man," yet you have no adult responsibilities or accountability to anyone? If so, how do you feel about that?

_____

_____

_____

_____

1.6 Can you think of any leadership qualities or skills you have? How are you demonstrating them? How are they affecting others?

_____

_____

_____

_____

1.7 What have you learned from reading this chapter that you didn't know before? How will you constructively apply your new knowledge?

_____

_____

_____

_____

-Additional Notes-

Reflections & Resolutions
"A Psalm to My Sons" by Dr. Rory Brown-Sipp

Life Lesson 1
Son, Father, Man, Christian, Leader

Resolutions

1A Based upon what you've read in this chapter, state one or more things you would like to change in certain areas of your life. What are you planning to do or change in order to improve?

_____

_____

_____

_____

1B What are some of the next steps you will commit to taking in order to become a more responsible, positive, contributing member of society?

_____

_____

_____

_____

1C After reading about leadership, do you believe you ought to develop any leadership skills you have and learn how to become a good leader? Why or why not? If so, what will you do to hone your skills?

_____

_____

_____

_____

-Additional Notes-

Reflections & Resolutions
"A Psalm to My Sons" by Dr. Rory Brown-Sipp

Life Lesson 2
Becoming Who You Are

Reflections

2.1 What initial thoughts did you have as you were reading this chapter?

_____
_____
_____
_____
_____

2.2 Which parts of this chapter's Life Lesson are the most significant to you? Which points are most useful for you? Why?

_____
_____
_____
_____
_____

2.3 Have you ever experienced anything similar to what you've read about in this chapter?

_____
_____
_____
_____
_____

2.4 Is someone close to you going through anything similar to what you've read in this chapter? If so, has this Life Lesson helped you understand that person's situation better? Do you believe you are likely to share any part of this Life Lesson with another person?

_____
_____
_____
_____

2.5 Have you ever faced rejection by someone you really cared for? How did you handle it? Is it still a problem for you?

_____
_____
_____
_____

2.6 What do others say when they compliment your specific and special qualities? How do you feel when you hear those comments? Which of your own qualities do you feel are the most positive?

_____
_____
_____
_____

2.7 Who are some of the people in your life who have helped shape your character and developed who you are as a person?

_____
_____
_____
_____

2.8 What have you learned from reading this chapter that you didn't know before? How will you constructively apply your new knowledge?

_____
_____
_____
_____

Reflections & Resolutions
"A Psalm to My Sons" by Dr. Rory Brown-Sipp

Life Lesson 2
Becoming Who You Are

Resolutions

2A Based upon what you've read in this chapter, state one or more things you would like to change in certain areas of your life. What are you planning to do or change in order to improve?

_____
_____
_____
_____

2B Is there anything about yourself physically that you didn't like but you will now accept—realizing it's better to be comfortable in your own skin than to put yourself down?

_____
_____
_____
_____

-Additional Notes-

-Additional Notes-

Reflections & Resolutions
"A Psalm to My Sons" by Dr. Rory Brown-Sipp

Life Lesson 3
Real Men and Boys Do Cry

Reflections

3.1 What initial thoughts did you have as you were reading this chapter?

3.2 Which parts of this chapter's Life Lesson are the most significant to you? Which points are most useful for you? Why?

3.3 Have you ever experienced anything similar to what you've read about in this chapter?

3.4 Is someone close to you going through anything similar to what you've read in this chapter? If so, has this Life Lesson helped you understand that person's situation better? Do you believe you are likely to share any part of this Life Lesson with another person?

3.5 How comfortable are you with crying and showing your sensitive emotions openly ?

3.6 Have you ever had to deal with ridicule from any members of your family, your peers, or any others for showing your emotions? If so, how did it make you feel?

3.7 What have you learned from reading this chapter that you didn't know before? How will you constructively apply your new knowledge?

-Additional Notes-

Reflections & Resolutions
"A Psalm to My Sons" by Dr. Rory Brown-Sipp

Life Lesson 3
Real Men and Boys Do Cry

Resolutions

3A Based upon what you've read in this chapter, state one or more things you would like to change in certain areas of your life. What are you planning to do or change in order to improve?

_____

_____

_____

_____

3B Can you think of anyone you may want or need to forgive for giving you a difficult time for showing your emotions? If so, how will you go about forgiving that person? How will you make peace within your mind about the situation?

_____

_____

_____

_____

-Additional Notes-

-Additional Notes-

Reflections & Resolutions
"A Psalm to My Sons" by Dr. Rory Brown-Sipp

Life Lesson 4
Keep Cool. Communicate. Live Violence-Free.

Reflections

4.1 What initial thoughts did you have as you were reading this chapter?

4.2 Which parts of this chapter's Life Lesson are the most significant to you? Which points are most useful for you? Why?

4.3 Have you ever experienced anything similar to what you've read about in this chapter?

4.4 Is someone close to you going through anything similar to what you've read in this chapter? If so, has this Life Lesson helped you understand that person's situation better? Do you believe you are likely to share any part of this Life Lesson with another person?

4.5 Do you often feel angry or upset about something someone says to you, says about you, or does around you? Do you find it is getting more difficult to deal with that situation? Can you calmly talk about it with that person? Will you? If not, why not?

_____
_____
_____
_____

4.6 Have you ever been faced with a confrontation in which you had to choose whether to remain or walk away when the situation was getting too intense or heated? What did you do and why?

_____
_____
_____
_____

4.7 What are some good ways to stay calm and keep a cool head when dealing with a conflict or physical confrontation?

_____
_____
_____
_____

4.8 What have you learned from reading this chapter that you didn't know before? How will you constructively apply your new knowledge?

_____
_____
_____
_____

Reflections & Resolutions
"A Psalm to My Sons" by Dr. Rory Brown-Sipp

Life Lesson 4
Keep Cool. Communicate. Live Violence-Free.

Resolutions

4A Based upon what you've read in this chapter, state one or more things you would like to change in certain areas of your life. What are you planning to do or change in order to improve?

_____
_____
_____
_____

4B List some things you are now going to do differently to ensure you are keeping yourself safe, healthy, and protected. How will you avoid placing yourself in unsafe, unhealthy situations or surroundings?

_____
_____
_____
_____

-Additional Notes-

-Additional Notes-

Reflections & Resolutions
"A Psalm to My Sons" by Dr. Rory Brown-Sipp

Life Lesson 5
Abstinence, Intimacy, and Avoiding "Baby Mama" Drama

Reflections

5.1 What initial thoughts did you have as you were reading this chapter?

5.2 Which parts of this chapter's Life Lesson are the most significant to you? Which points are most useful for you? Why?

5.3 Have you ever experienced anything similar to what you've read about in this chapter?

5.4 Is someone close to you going through anything similar to what you've read in this chapter? If so, has this Life Lesson helped you understand that person's situation better? Do you believe you are likely to share any part of this Life Lesson with another person?

5.5 Can you think of ways that you can show your partner that you care but without becoming prematurely involved in intimate, sexual interaction that could lead to an unplanned pregnancy or other problems?

5.6 When you think about your future, can you see how unwise decisions you may have made in your youth can cause financial problems for many years to come? Can you see how your life may be diminished in other ways by making poor, unwise decisions today?

5.7 What have you learned from reading this chapter that you didn't know before? How will you constructively apply your new knowledge?

-Additional Notes-

Reflections & Resolutions
"A Psalm to My Sons" by Dr. Rory Brown-Sipp

Life Lesson 5
Abstinence, Intimacy, and Avoiding "Baby Mama" Drama

Resolutions

5A Based upon what you've read in this chapter, state one or more things you would like to change in certain areas of your life. What are you planning to do or change in order to improve?

_____
_____
_____
_____

5B Have you ever made decisions too quickly or were too impatient to wait before taking an action and later regretted it? List ways that you can avoid doing that. How will you practice better decision-making in your life?

_____
_____
_____
_____

-Additional Notes-

-Additional Notes-

Reflections & Resolutions
"A Psalm to My Sons" by Dr. Rory Brown-Sipp

Life Lesson 6
Education, Enterprise, and Empowerment

Reflections

6.1 What initial thoughts did you have as you were reading this chapter?

_____
_____
_____
_____

6.2 Which parts of this chapter's Life Lesson are the most significant to you? Which points are most useful for you? Why?

_____
_____
_____
_____

6.3 Have you ever experienced anything similar to what you've read about in this chapter?

_____
_____
_____

6.4 Is someone close to you going through anything similar to what you've read in this chapter? If so, has this Life Lesson helped you understand that person's situation better? Do you believe you are likely to share any part of this Life Lesson with another person?

_____
_____
_____

6.5 When you think about your future, do you see yourself in a particular type of career, job, or position in a company? Why or why not?

_____
_____
_____
_____
_____

6.6 Can you think of any leadership qualities or skills you have? How are you demonstrating them? How are they affecting the others?

_____
_____
_____
_____

6.7 After reading about the PAID Life System, can you think of any areas of your life where the four practices—perseverance, accessing, investment, and determination—would help you improve or achieve your goals? What are some of those areas?

_____
_____
_____
_____

6.8 What have you learned from reading this chapter that you didn't know before? How will you constructively apply your new knowledge?

_____
_____
_____
_____
_____
_____

Reflections & Resolutions
"A Psalm to My Sons" by Dr. Rory Brown-Sipp

Life Lesson 6
Education, Enterprise, and Empowerment

Resolutions

6A When you think about your future, do you see yourself in a particular type of career, job, or position in a company? Why or why not?

_____
_____
_____
_____

6B Write a statement that describes what you plan to be doing one month from now to further your education goals or to advance in your income-earning power. One year from now? Five years from now?

_____
_____
_____
_____
_____

-Additional Notes-

-Additional Notes-

Reflections & Resolutions
"A Psalm to My Sons" by Dr. Rory Brown-Sipp

Life Lesson 7
The Gift of Christ

Reflections

7.1 What initial thoughts did you have as you were reading this chapter?

7.2 Which parts of this chapter's Life Lesson are the most significant to you? Which points are most useful for you? Why?

7.3 Have you ever experienced anything similar to what you've read about in this chapter?

7.4 Is someone close to you going through anything similar to what you've read in this chapter? If so, has this Life Lesson helped you understand that person's situation better? Do you believe you are likely to share any part of this Life Lesson with another person?

7.5 Has anyone close to you helped you grow spiritually? If so, in what ways were you helped? Do you believe you are growing toward a more fulfilling relationship with God or a power you consider to be greater than yourself?

_____
_____
_____
_____

7.6 Do you believe you have spiritual gifts that you can use in your life? What are they? How do they help you and others close to you? What other constructive ways can you use those gifts?

_____
_____
_____
_____
_____

7.7 What have you learned from reading this chapter that you didn't know before? How will you constructively apply your new knowledge?

_____
_____
_____
_____

-Additional Notes-

Reflections & Resolutions
"A Psalm to My Sons" by Dr. Rory Brown-Sipp

Life Lesson 7
The Gift of Christ

Resolutions

7A Based upon what you've read in this chapter, state one or more things you would like to change in certain areas of your life. What are you planning to do or change in order to improve?

_____
_____
_____
_____

7B If you accept that your body is your temple, how can you use that awareness to your own benefit? In what ways will you work to preserve your physical well-being? List anything you will begin to do differently to care for your body in a healthier manner.

_____
_____
_____
_____

-Additional Notes-

STAY CONNECTED

Thank you for your interest in *A Psalm to My Sons*.
You may contact the author with your comments or questions via the website www.APsalmToMySons.com and links to social media sites.

Whenever posting online, please use privacy and safety precautions.
If you are under 18, ask for a parent's or guardian's permission or help to go on to the Internet.

Post no identifying personal information online that reveals your full identity, address, family members, neighborhood, school, or workplace, and so forth.

Need Help?

In the event you are experiencing any situation that requires immediate assistance, contact a trusted family member or a responsible adult such as a school counselor.

If you are in physical danger, being threatened or bullied, living in an unsafe, unhealthy situation, or if you believe you may be the victim of a crime, contact your local law enforcement agency or police department immediately. Ask for help.

Dial 911
Police Department - Emergency
or check the local phone listings

Dial 311
Police Department – Dispatch for Non-emergency
or check the local phone listings

-See the Following Pages for Other Helpful Resources-

www.APsalmToMySons.com

Visit the website for other resources, updates, and to obtain downloadable "Reflections & Resolutions" worksheets.

Also, reproductions of chapter artwork are available for purchase online. See page 123 for Gallery of Illustrations.

Dr. Rory Brown-Sipp is a Southern Nevada-based author, executive director of a federally funded program, early childhood education expert, university professor, and Christian leader.

He is available for consulting and speaking engagements.

RESOURCES
Southern Nevada

ACELERO LEARNING
Early Childhood Education - "Head Start" Program
www.acelero.net

SERENITY
Community Care & Behavioral Health Services
www.serenitylasvegas.com

EISTEAM Community Wellness Centers
www.EISTEAMCWC.com

RESOURCES
National

The following is a list of organizations and public, state, or federal agencies. This is provided as reference only for readers who may need to seek assistance or support with certain vital concerns or general matters.

If you or someone you know is experiencing a medical or safety crisis or any emergency, immediately notify the appropriate authorities or dial local police at 911. Get help.

Dial 211
(Not all states participate)
Website: www.211.org
Nationwide helpline for connecting to local area and state resources for help with issues under the categories of health care, personal safety, child protection, family planning, drug and alcohol intervention, problem gambling, job training, reading literacy, education, and many others.

Boys Town National Hotline
1-800-448-3000 Toll-Free
24-Hours, 7 Days a Week, 365 Days a Year
Over 20 years of helping boys and families
www.BoysTown.org

Crisis Call Center
1-800-273-8255 Toll-Free
Support and assistance in times of trouble
www.CrisisCallCenter.org

National Domestic Violence Hotline
1-800-799-SAFE (799-7233)
24-Hours, 7 Days a Week
(800) 787-3224 (TTY)
www.NDVH.org

Planned Parenthood National Hotline
1-800-230-PLAN (7526)
24-Hours, 7 Days a Week
For Routing to Local Resources
www.PlannedParenthood.org

GLBT National Youth Talkline
1-800-246-PRIDE (7743)
4 p.m. – 12 a.m. EST, Mon - Fri
www.glnh.org/talkline

National Suicide Hotline
1-800-SUICIDE (784-2433)
1-800-HOPE (4673)
24-Hours, 7 Days a Week
www.Hopeline.com

National Teen Dating Abuse Hotline
1-866-331-9474 Toll-Free
24-Hours, 7 Days a Week
www.LoveIsRespect.org

1-800-THE-LOST
Missing and kidnapped children; sex trafficking; youth sexual exploitation, victim and family support
www.MissingKids.com

CyberTipline
1-800-843-5678
Crime prevention and reporting suspected child abuse online (The CyberTipline is operated in partnership with the FBI, Immigration and Customs Enforcement, U.S. Postal Inspection Service, U.S. Secret Service, military criminal investigative organizations, U.S. Department of Justice, Internet Crimes Against Children Task Force program, as well as other state and local law enforcement agencies.)

GALLERY

Illustrations at the opening of each chapter were all inspired by the author, Dr. Rory Brown-Sipp, and created by the artist, Ricky Scott Holmes.

Prints suitable for framing can be ordered online.

Visit **www.APsalmToMySons.com** for a link to the Art Gallery to order reproductions in a choice of print sizes.

1.

2.
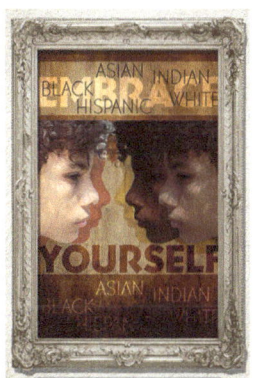

3.

4.
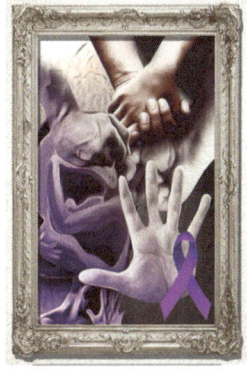

5.

6.

7.

Chapter 1: "Heritage"

Chapter 2: "Reflections"

Chapter 3: "Boys Do Cry"

Chapter 4: "H.O.P.E. - Hands of Peace & Empathy"

Chapter 5: "Intimacy"

Chapter 6: "Two Roads, One Dream"

Chapter 7: "The Gift"

Illustrator - Ricky Scott Holmes   Copyright 2014. By Dr. Rory Brown-Sipp. All Rights Reserved.

www.ingramcontent.com/pod-product-compliance
Lightning Source LLC
Chambersburg PA
CBHW041616220426
43671CB00001B/10